# THE
# GOSPEL ACCORDING TO
# MARK

COMMENTARY BY

## C.F.D. MOULE

*Emeritus Lady Margaret's Professor of Divinity
in the University of Cambridge*

## CAMBRIDGE UNIVERSITY PRESS

CAMBRIDGE

LONDON · NEW YORK · MELBOURNE

Published by the Syndics of the Cambridge University Press
The Pitt Building, Trumpington Street, Cambridge CB2 1RP
Bentley House, 200 Euston Road, London NW1 2DB
32 East 57th Street, New York, NY 10022, USA
296 Beaconsfield Parade, Middle Park, Melbourne 3206, Australia

Library of Congress catalogue card number: 65–19152

ISBN 0 521 04210 0 hard covers
ISBN 0 521 09288 4 paperback

First published 1965
Reprinted with corrections 1969 1972
Reprinted 1975 1977 1978

Printed in Great Britain at the
University Press, Cambridge

# GENERAL EDITORS' PREFACE

The aim of this series is to provide the text of the New English Bible closely linked to a commentary in which the results of modern scholarship are made available to the general reader. Teachers and young people preparing for such examinations as the General Certificate of Education at Ordinary or Advanced Level in Britain, and similar qualifications elsewhere have been especially kept in mind. The commentators have been asked to assume no specialized theological knowledge, and no knowledge of Greek and Hebrew. Bare references to other literature and multiple references to other parts of the Bible have been avoided. Actual quotations have been given as often as possible.

Within these quite severe limits each commentator will attempt to set out the main findings of recent New Testament scholarship, and to describe the historical background to the text. The main theological content of the New Testament will also be critically discussed.

Much attention has been given to the form of the volumes. The aim is to produce books each of which will be read consecutively from first to last page. The introductory material leads naturally into the text, which itself leads into the alternating sections of commentary. By this means it is hoped that each book will be easily read and remain in the mind as a unity.

The series will be prefaced by a volume—*Understanding the New Testament*—which will outline the larger historical background, say something about the growth and transmission of the text, and answer the question 'Why should we study the New Testament?' Another volume—*New Testament Illustrations*—will contain maps, diagrams and photographs.

P. R. A.

A. R. C. L.

J. W. P.

# COMMENTATOR'S PREFACE

This small book contains one or two ideas that, I think, are more or less original; but, in the main, it owes so much to others that, if the normal method of acknowledgement had been adopted, it would have consisted largely of footnotes. As it is, footnotes have been banned, with a view to the comfort of the reader; and I can only ask the living scholars whose ideas have been quietly pillaged to believe that I am at least a grateful thief, although, like most thieves, I do not advertise the robbery. As for the scholars who are no longer living, perhaps they have some more direct way of knowing my indebtedness and gratitude.

But to the General Editors of this series at least I can tender my thanks by name. I cannot be grateful enough to Professor P. R. Ackroyd, Dr A. R. C. Leaney, and Mr J. W. Packer for their generous help in reading drafts and sending in detailed comments, and for their patience and courtesy. No commentary on Mark's Gospel, on whatever scale, could be worthy—that goes without saying; but without the help and encouragement of the Editors, this little commentary would be much poorer than it is. To my Secretary, Mrs Willetts, go first-class honours for deciphering unpromising scripts and patiently re-typing alterations; and to the Cambridge University Press my thanks for expert assistance.

C.F.D.M.

# CONTENTS

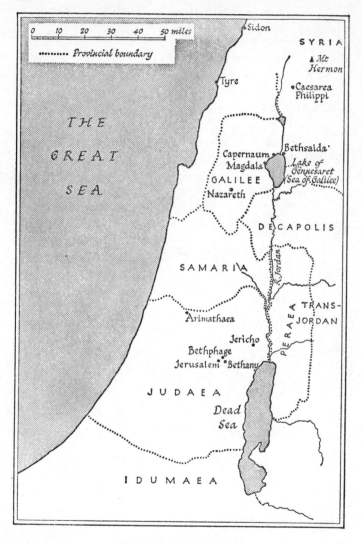

MAP OF PALESTINE

x

# THE GOSPEL ACCORDING TO

# MARK

✻  ✻  ✻  ✻  ✻  ✻  ✻  ✻  ✻  ✻  ✻  ✻  ✻

## WHAT SORT OF A BOOK IS IT?

'The Gospel according to Mark' is a title that has been added
to this book from very early days; but in itself the book is
anonymous: the writer says nothing whatever about himself.
The meagre evidence about its origin will be quoted later.
Much more important is the question, What is this little
book, and what does it contain?

The Christian Church began its existence simply as a hand-
ful of people bearing witness to something that they were
convinced had happened. They had experienced it, and they
were still experiencing it. They called it good news, or, in
Greek, *euangelion* (evangel). The old English word used for
this is gospel.

Here is an example, from Acts 10: 38–43, of the kind of
thing they said when they were announcing this good news—
this gospel:

'You know about Jesus of Nazareth, how God anointed
him with the Holy Spirit and with power. He went about
doing good and healing all who were oppressed by the devil,
for God was with him. And we can bear witness to all that he
did in the Jewish country-side and in Jerusalem. He was put
to death by hanging on a gibbet; but God raised him to life on
the third day, and allowed him to appear, not to the whole
people, but to witnesses whom God had chosen in advance—
to us, who ate and drank with him after he rose from the dead.
He commanded us to proclaim him to the people, and affirm
that he is the one who has been designated by God as judge
of the living and the dead. It is to him that all the prophets

testify, declaring that everyone who trusts in him receives forgiveness of sins through his name.'

It was easy enough to expand such an outline of the good news, because there were many anecdotes and sayings of Jesus circulating among his friends. These would be told as occasion arose, to meet difficulties, or to answer critics, or simply because they were interesting; and they had probably begun to be written down separately at a very early date. But Mark's book is one of the earliest examples—perhaps positively the earliest—of an arrangement of these units of tradition into a connected whole.

It is not merely a collection of the sayings of Jesus; indeed, it has more narratives than sayings. But neither is it a life of Jesus, like a modern biography. It is a piecing together of stories and sayings in such a way that they constitute an announcement of 'the good news'. There is no other word for it, therefore, than the gospel—the good news—as Mark tells it, or according to Mark.

It presents its brief anecdotes with impressive directness and simplicity and swiftness. Without any preliminary account of Jesus's birth and childhood, it plunges straight into the story by introducing John the Baptist and recounting how Jesus came to him for baptism. Then, in quick succession, specimens are given of what Jesus did and said, of how the crowds responded but the religious leaders resented him, and of how he trained his small band of close friends and followers. About two-fifths of the whole book is devoted to the closing days of his life; and then the narrative breaks off abruptly at the empty tomb. What follows (16: 9 ff.) is a summary of the traditions about the subsequent events. It is generally recognized that this is a later addition, patched on by some other writer; but it was early enough, even so, to get into the Gospel in its accepted form.

Thus Mark is a little handbook for basic Christian instruction, simple, yet brilliantly dramatic—a stark, powerful presentation of the Christian facts: not a biography, but a portrait of Jesus as the one who not only proclaimed but somehow brought with him the kingdom of God. Here is far more than a martyr; here is the triumphant and victorious Son of God. The book was probably written for the leader of some Christian community, to help him in teaching his people and in explaining to inquirers what Christians believed. It may well have been some time before there were enough copies of it to distribute to the leaders of other communities—let alone enough for individuals to possess for themselves. Every copy of a book had to be laboriously produced by hand, and even papyrus, the paper of those days, was not always easy to obtain in quantity.

## SOME OF ITS CHARACTERISTICS

An important part of the study of the Christian good news is to compare with one another the presentations of it by Matthew, Mark, and Luke. John's version of the Gospel, too, has to be brought in, but his treatment of it sets his book in a special class. Matthew, Mark, and Luke can be most easily compared by using a 'synopsis'—a book which prints the three in parallel columns. The present commentary, however, makes no attempt to do this work of comparison systematically. It is designed, rather, to help you, by explanations and comments, to understand Mark's book in itself. But first, an excellent thing to do is to read Mark straight through at a sitting (it is very short, and even to read it aloud with a group of friends only takes about an hour and a half). If you do this, you can hardly fail to be impressed. Papias, a writer of about A.D. 130, who will be mentioned again shortly, said that Mark's writing was 'not in order'. Whatever he may have meant by that, the arrangement is, in fact, remarkably skilful —some even think that Mark used an elaborate patterning to convey his theological meaning; and, although his Greek is colloquial, the total effect is of extraordinary vividness and dramatic vigour, only enhanced by the restraint and reticence and complete self-effacement of the writer himself.

His story is unadorned and unpretentious, but quite over-powering. It moves with extraordinary rapidity. It vividly sketches in the character of Jesus—strong and without senti-mentality, yet gentle and sensitive and tender. But, above all, this is clearly a story, not merely of a wonderful, human life, but of the irresistible, irreversible movement of a divine plan, leading up to an astonishing climax—the empty tomb! And, if you want to bring home to yourself its naturalness and reality, you only have to contrast it with the shallow romances which, quite soon, began to compete (fortunately, without much success) with the Gospels we now have in the New Testament. Such romances may be read in M. R. James's *The Apocryphal New Testament* (1924) or in *New Testament Apocrypha*, translated by R. McL. Wilson, 1963.

By comparison, the dignity, the simplicity, the convincing directness of Mark are vastly impressive. The whole story takes place within a tiny country and in the space of a few years; but its meaning is infinite.

## THE AUTHOR

And now, what is known about the origin of this astonishing little book?

In about A.D. 320, Eusebius, bishop of Caesarea, wrote in Greek a history of the Church. Eusebius reports that Papias, who was bishop of Hierapolis in Asia Minor in about A.D. 130, had recorded a tradition that Mark's Gospel was a translation into Greek of the teaching which the apostle Peter had given in Rome. Peter himself, then, presumably used Hebrew, or Aramaic (a language similar to Hebrew) and addressed groups of Jews who used these languages. It is generally assumed that the Mark who wrote the Gospel was the young man called John Mark in Acts (12: 12, 25; 15: 37, 39), who was indeed a companion of the apostles. This identification is not inevitable —Marcus was not an uncommon name—and the degree of this Gospel's attachment to the body of traditional information

4

about Peter has been questioned. But parts of it do, in fact, read like a direct, eyewitness account; and a recently discovered copy of what seems to be a genuine letter of Clement of Alexandria (about A.D. 190), also speaks definitely of Peter's notes as forming part of Mark's material.

Mark is very widely believed to have been written earlier than Matthew or Luke, but much hard thinking about this question is still going on, and rather startling new ideas may yet emerge. On any showing, however, Mark's Gospel is separated from the events it describes by, at most, a generation —perhaps less. Peter was martyred round about A.D. 60. Even if the Gospel was put together after that, it is not much later. At the latest, it cannot have been written more than some thirty to thirty-five years after the death of Jesus; and the traditions it draws on take us, in some cases, right back to the very words of Jesus himself.

The newly discovered letter of Clement of Alexandria, already alluded to, declares that, besides the Gospel which we know, Mark wrote another, expanded version, containing more mystical material for the exclusive use of those who had made progress in the Christian life. He even quotes two sections purporting to come from this secret, 'mystic' Mark. Despite Clement's statement, it is doubtful whether it is authentic Mark that he quotes—any more than 16: 9–20 are authentic (see notes there). But this is, at any rate, an interesting addition to the traditions.

## THEOLOGICAL QUESTIONS

Many theological and ethical questions of front-rank importance are raised in Mark's small book. So far as possible, these are discussed in the commentary. The following list shows where the main discussions occur:

Allegory and parable, 32 f., 56, 93 f.
Apocalypse, 101 ff.
Apostles, 30 f.
Authority, 22, 73, 93

✻ ✻ ✻ ✻ ✻ ✻ ✻ ✻ ✻ ✻ ✻ ✻ ✻

# The Coming of Christ

### THE FORERUNNER'S CALL TO PENITENCE; HIS WITNESS

HERE BEGINS THE GOSPEL of Jesus Christ the Son 1 of God.

In the prophet Isaiah it stands written: 'Here is my 2 herald whom I send on ahead of you, and he will prepare your way. A voice crying aloud in the wilderness, 3 "Prepare a way for the Lord; clear a straight path for him." And so it was that John the Baptist appeared in 4 the wilderness proclaiming a baptism in token of repentance, for the forgiveness of sins; and they flocked to him 5 from the whole Judaean country-side and the city of Jerusalem, and were baptized by him in the River Jordan, confessing their sins.

6 John was dressed in a rough coat of camel's hair, with a leather belt round his waist, and he fed on locusts and
7 wild honey. His proclamation ran: 'After me comes one who is mightier than I. I am not fit to unfasten his shoes.
8 I have baptized you with water; he will baptize you with the Holy Spirit.'

* I. *Here begins the Gospel.* As we have seen (pp. I-2) Mark's book has come to be called *a* Gospel because it contains *the* Gospel—the announcement of the Christian good news. It is this latter meaning of Gospel that is here intended. The starting-point of this good news is defined in Acts I: 22: it is 'from John's ministry of baptism...'; and again, in Matt. II: 12, Luke 16: 16 and John I: 6, John the Baptist is taken as the starting-point. So here in Mark, it is John with whom the story begins.

2-5. John's preaching *in the wilderness* is itself treated as a sign that he is the destined forerunner of some special action on the part of God, because it links him with a well-known passage in the Old Testament which expressed confidence that God was going to take such action. Isa. 40: 3 says: 'There is a voice that cries: Prepare a road for the LORD through the wilderness, clear a highway across the desert for our God.' It was easy, in the original Hebrew or in the Greek version, to read 'through (literally in) the wilderness' as though it went with 'cries', and thus corresponded to John's situation. The recently discovered Dead Sea Scrolls provide evidence for a Jewish monastic community in the barren, rocky land between Jerusalem and the Dead Sea who applied this same quotation to themselves, and it is possible that John may himself have been associated with them (see Luke I: 80, 'he lived out in the wilds until the day when he appeared publicly...'). If so, he very literally appeared *in the wilderness*, though the Greek word *erēmos*, here translated wilderness, does not everywhere in the Gospels seem to mean more than the uncultivated land outside towns. The corresponding word in the Old Testament indicates 'pasture-land', the areas in which the flocks were led by the shepherds.

The other Old Testament quotation, *Here is my herald whom I send on ahead of you* (verse 2), comes, not from Isaiah at all, but from Mal. 3: 1 ('Look, I am sending my messenger...', though Exod. 23: 20 has it also, for 'angel' there is the same, in Hebrew, as 'messenger'). The fact that the two quotations are both ascribed to Isaiah may mean that they occurred side by side under a single heading in some collection of prophecies. About the meaning of the Malachi passage (including Mal. 4: 5), see the comment on 9: 2–8 below.

4. There has been much discussion of the origin and meaning of John the Baptist's baptism. Bathing or sprinkling with water is a very widespread religious symbol for purification. Within Judaism, the Dead Sea sect just mentioned seems to have used it frequently; and bathing in water is known, at least later, if not already by the time of the Baptist, to have been part of the ceremony by which a Gentile convert to Judaism was admitted into the community of Israel. Besides this, sprinkling with clean water was already familiar from Ezek. 36: 25 etc. as a figurative expression for the moral cleansing of the nation by God: '...I will sprinkle clean water over you, and you shall be clean from all that defiles you; I will cleanse you from the taint of all your idols.' Thus, the Baptist, who was so called because of his symbolic use of water, was in this way evidently giving dramatic, visible expression to his call to repentance. Those whose consciences responded to John's call to moral reform submitted to being dipped in the river—John had come from 'the wilderness' to the River Jordan for the purpose—as a sign of their response. Luke 3: 7–14 gives some account of the sort of sins of which he summoned his hearers to repent.

6–8. But this rugged prophet not only called for moral reform: he announced that someone infinitely greater was to follow him and that he would baptize with the Holy Spirit.

John's mission was thus essentially a preparation for something greater still. The Jewish historian Josephus, in the *Antiquities of the Jews* (Book XVIII, 116–19), written about A.D. 93, describes John as baptizing, and preaching morals. He is silent about this other side of his message, except that, in noting that Herod executed John as a potential revolutionary, Josephus bears indirect witness to a message concerned with Israelite nationalist hopes. John was a preacher of morals, but had a message also for Israel's future. There is more about John the Baptist in 6: 14–29.

Baptism *with the Holy Spirit* is a striking phrase. The Holy Spirit is God himself at work among his people, and it is impossible for a person literally to have the Holy Spirit poured over him like water. But the Baptist evidently meant that the great coming One would not merely cleanse with water but would bring to bear, like a deluge, the purging, purifying, judging presence of God himself. Christians, looking back on these events, often contrasted John's water-baptism with this even more powerful purging and refining—this smelting fire. In Acts 1: 5 the risen Christ says: 'John, as you know, baptized with water, but you will be baptized with the Holy Spirit...'; so, in Rom. 8: 9, St Paul says outright: 'if a man does not possess the Spirit of Christ, he is no Christian'. In Acts 2: 1 ff. the beginning of the Church's active life is marked by dramatic signs of the coming of the Spirit; and this is hailed (Acts 2: 16 ff.) as the fulfilment of Old Testament expectation as expressed in Joel 2: 28 ff.: 'Thereafter the day shall come when I will pour out my spirit on all mankind...I will show portents in the sky and on earth, blood and fire and columns of smoke...' Thus John the Baptist's baptism was recognized as marking the threshold of the kingdom of God, but not the full entry into it. As Jesus said, 'the least in the kingdom of Heaven is greater than he' (Matt. 11: 11; cf. Luke 7: 28). ✳

## THE BAPTISM AND TESTING OF JESUS

It happened at this time that Jesus came from Nazareth in 9
Galilee and was baptized in the Jordan by John. At the 10
moment when he came up out of the water, he saw the
heavens torn open and the Spirit, like a dove, descending
upon him. And a voice spoke from heaven: 'Thou art 11
my Son, my Beloved; on thee my favour rests.'

Thereupon the Spirit sent him away into the wilderness, 12
and there he remained for forty days tempted by Satan. 13
He was among the wild beasts; and the angels waited on
him.

✻ Jesus began his public career in this very humble way, by
accepting baptism at the hands of John. But with it came a
special experience—the conviction that, in a unique sense, he
was God's own Son; and instantly, on the heels of it, follows a
prolonged testing by 'the Opposition'. That is what the word
Satan means in Hebrew; but it had come to be virtually a
proper name for the Chief Enemy of God, the Devil (which is
a Greek word, also used in the New Testament, for the one
who slanders or misrepresents). Matthew and Luke go into
more detail about this testing, and show it as a direct challenge
to Jesus to doubt or to misuse his position as Son of God. The
whole Gospel story can be seen as a picture of Jesus working
out this sonship day by day in terms of eager obedience to the
plan of God—an obedience which, in the end, leads to death.
So the baptism and testing of Jesus together strike the note, at
the very beginning of the story, of unswerving, dedicated
loyalty. *Jesus...the Son of God* is the theme of the beginning
and end of Mark (1: 1; 15: 39).

11. It is often said that *Thou art my Son, my Beloved; on thee
my favour rests* is a combination, in the consciousness of Jesus,
of two famous Old Testament phrases: 'You are my son',

from Ps. 2: 7; and the reference to God's dedicated Servant in Isa. 42: 1 as 'my chosen one in whom I delight'. There is no doubt that Jesus does combine the two roles of Son and suffering Servant, and, indeed, that he interprets the one by the other. But whether this particular combination of texts is intended is less clear, as well as less important. The mysterious divine voice, declaring Jesus 'Son', is going to be heard again, at 9: 7.

It is noteworthy that all Christians, like Jesus himself, though with much less intensity and absoluteness, have to face the same testing that comes when they are made children of God: 'Is it real?' the tempter asks; or, 'If it is real, why not use it to satisfy your own desire for power?' Jesus's interpretation of sonship in terms of obedience to God and service to men is a profound insight into the answers to the tempter's questions.

*the heavens torn open, the wild beasts,* and *the angels*: we need not prosaically try either to explain these or to explain them away. Such language is almost the only possible way of speaking of experiences too deep to be recorded in mere prose and too real to be ignored—the sense of tremendous urgency, the sense of loneliness and terror, and the sense that, after all, God has not forgotten. ✻

# In Galilee: Success and Opposition

### THE GOSPEL; THE FIRST COMPANIONS SUMMONED

14  AFTER JOHN had been arrested, Jesus came into Galilee
15  proclaiming the Gospel of God: 'The time has come; the kingdom of God is upon you; repent, and believe the Gospel.'

Jesus was walking by the Sea of Galilee when he 16 saw Simon and his brother Andrew on the lake at work with a casting-net; for they were fishermen. Jesus said 17 to them, 'Come with me, and I will make you fishers of men.' And at once they left their nets and followed 18 him.

When he had gone a little further he saw James son of 19 Zebedee and his brother John, who were in the boat over-hauling their nets. He called them; and, leaving their 20 father Zebedee in the boat with the hired men, they went off to follow him.

\* 14. *After John had been arrested* is an anticipation of the story told in 6: 14–29. The phrase suggests that Jesus was careful not to exercise his ministry in rivalry to the Baptist's, but saw himself as, in a sense, John's successor. John, as we have seen, looked for a successor; but he knew that this successor would not be a disciple merely, but someone incomparably greater than he.

15. The message of Jesus is tersely summarized: *The time has come; the kingdom of God is upon you; repent, and believe the Gospel.*

*The time has come* meant that, after centuries of waiting and expectancy on the part of the Jews, at last the climax had been reached.

God had often been spoken of in the Old Testament as the King of Israel; and Israel, in a special sense, was his own people. And even when the monarchy was well established, it was still recognized that the human king ruled in the name of God. There are several Psalms which begin with the cry, 'The LORD is king' (e.g. Pss. 93, 97, 99). Thus, the ideal future for Israel was often pictured as a time when God's reign would be fully acknowledged; and sometimes it was thought of as ushered in by an ideal representative ruler—the anointed one (Hebrew: *Messiah*; Greek: *Christ*), that is, a king duly acknowledged by the religious ritual of pouring over him the sacred perfumed oil. About Messiah more will be said at 8: 27 — 9: 1.

So now the moment had come for God's special action. What was this action to be? It was to be the bringing of God's sovereignty to bear on Israel, and, through Israel, on the world. Jesus called for willingness to change direction (*repent*), in view of the good news (*Gospel*) that the reign (*kingdom*) of God was close at hand. God's sovereignty, this seems to say, is about to be shown them in a new way; and the people needed to change their ideas and change their way of life—to turn round from their self-centred concerns so as to face and accept God's kingship as it came among them. The rest of the Gospel, it might be said, consists of illustrations of the way in which the deeds and words and character of Jesus himself brought this sovereignty of God to bear on his people. Wherever he was, there people found themselves confronted with the 'kingdom of God'; and, although Jesus himself seems to have pointed forwards to events that were to happen before the kingship of God was fully recognized, yet clearly to this extent, it had begun to come already. See further the note on 9: 1.

16–20. Two pairs of fishermen brothers are summoned by Jesus to leave their trade and go with him. Hitherto they had caught fish: Jesus would enlist them among his helpers as *fishers of men*. We must not press the metaphor, so as to think of bait and nets: the fisherman, it is true, catches fish in order to eat them; but the evangelist catches men for their own salvation as well as for the good of others. All four brothers appear among the twelve companions of Jesus in 3: 13–19. There is another similar summons coming at 2: 14; but Jesus did not call everybody to abandon his former occupation or settled life. In 5: 18–19 he expressly forbids a man he has cured to come with him, but sends him back to his own town; and Jesus must have preached to thousands without intending that they should give up their ordinary work. But we hear of the few who are called away; and they remind us that nobody can enter the kingdom of God without being so dedicated to God where he is that he is *ready* to go anywhere and part with anything. The claims of discipleship are expressed uncompromisingly in 8: 34–5: 'Anyone who wishes to be a follower of mine must leave self behind. . . . ' *

### STORIES OF CURES: I: 2I — 2: I2

* One of the most striking features of Jesus's life was the cure, without medicine or surgery, of countless people who were ill. This is referred to, in one way or another, not only in Mark, but also in material used exclusively in the Gospel according to Luke, and in Acts 10: 38; also in anti-Christian statements in rabbinic writings and by Celsus, the opponent of Christianity to whom the great Christian scholar Origen wrote a reply in his *contra Celsum*, about A.D. 245.

Thus we are confronted with what is generally called 'the miraculous'. Actually, the original Greek of the New Testament does not generally use any equivalent word although the English versions find it difficult to avoid. 'Miracle', strictly, means something to be wondered or surprised at; and, although the crowds are often said to have been surprised or amazed, what Jesus did is mostly called not 'a miracle'—a merely marvellous thing—but an act of power, *dunamis*, or, in John's Gospel, a sign, *semeion*.

It seems that, wherever Jesus went, surprising things did happen. But the importance of them lay not in their marvellous quality: they were not, like conjuring tricks, merely astonishing; nor were they ever done merely in order to surprise. They always seem to have been the result, simply, of Jesus's concern for people and his perfect and absolute obedience, as Son of God, to the will of his Father. We assume, quite correctly, that there is a regularity and consistency about nature, and that effect can always be relied upon to follow cause, so that, when the spark reaches the gunpowder, there is bound to be a bang. What we forget is that we have never ourselves witnessed a situation in which persons needing help are reached by a man quite perfectly in line with God's will, as Jesus was according to the New Testament. Might it not be that what we call a miracle would be the natural and inevitable effect, given such a cause, and given also enough of what the Gospels call faith—trust in God—on the part of the other persons concerned? That is why these miracles are called acts of power: they are natural phenomena, whenever the power of God is let through by obedience and concern for persons and by a readiness to trust God.

Even in the presence of Jesus, this kind of thing did not happen everywhere. It involves a personal relationship, and where the response is lacking, there Jesus cannot forcibly impose the will of God: that would be contrary to God's own character and his respect for human freedom. In Mark 6: 5–6 we read: 'He could work no miracle [act of power] there, except that he put his hands on a few sick people and healed them; and he was taken aback by their want of faith.' And today, the same principle holds good. Lack of faith and lack of obedience set up barriers. But very striking things happen where men will fully accept the will of God and put themselves at his disposal, seeking not the sense of power for its own sake, but the glory of God.

Such deeds of power as Jesus worked, and such as God still works where he is fully trusted and obeyed, are enough to serve as signs that, where God's sovereignty is really acknowledged, there evil begins to be brought under control. The life and work of Jesus were a great battle against 'the Opposition' (see note on verses 9–13 above); the deeds of power are preliminary signs of the outcome of that campaign. *

### THE MAN POSSESSED BY AN UNCLEAN SPIRIT

They came to Capernaum, and on the Sabbath he went to 21
synagogue and began to teach. The people were astounded 22
at his teaching, for, unlike the doctors of the law, he
taught with a note of authority. Now there was a man 23
in the synagogue possessed by an unclean spirit. He
shrieked: 'What do you want with us, Jesus of Naza- 24
reth? Have you come to destroy us? I know who you are
—the Holy One of God.' Jesus rebuked him: 'Be silent', 25
he said, 'and come out of him.' And the unclean spirit 26
threw the man into convulsions and with a loud cry left
him. They were all dumbfounded and began to ask one 27
another, 'What is this? A new kind of teaching! He
speaks with authority. When he gives orders, even the
unclean spirits submit.' The news spread rapidly, and he 28
was soon spoken of all over the district of Galilee.

\* This particular cure is an instance of what is called exorcism
—that is the expulsion of a demon from a person by an author-
itative word of command. The idea that a demon had taken
possession of a person was the explanation commonly given
in those days, as it still is in some parts of the world today, for
symptoms which modern medical science would describe in
terms of mental or even physical illness. It does not make a
great deal of difference, because the mental or physical condition also—madness, or paralysis, or whatever it may be—is
ultimately due to a situation in which opposition to God's will
has got the upper hand. This does not, of course, mean necessarily that the individual sufferer has deliberately surrendered to
evil, though that may sometimes be the case. It means, more
often, that evil has got into the whole human society, making
broken homes and false relationships and setting up tensions

where there should be harmonious co-operation. In the presence of the Son of God, such evil finds words (as happens again at 3: 11): it cries out in hatred and alarm: *What do you want with us...?...I know who you are—the Holy One of God.* Jesus, with absolute confidence and mastery, asserts the will of God—and the Opposition caves in.

21. *the Sabbath* was the seventh day of the week, a day of worship, and, in this respect, though not in all respects, like Christian Sunday. See note on verse 32.

*went to synagogue.* Synagogues must be carefully distinguished from the temple. Apart from possible rivals in Egypt, there was only one temple for all Jews. Here the great annual festivals were celebrated with chanting and ritual, animals were slaughtered in sacrifice, and other offerings were presented, under the direction of large numbers of priests in their rotas of duty (see note on 11: 15–19 below). But there were synagogues in plenty all over the empire—in big towns there would be several. Here, on Saturdays, the Scriptures were read and expounded and prayer was offered. And the synagogue, or rooms adjoining it, served also as a school, and seems to have been a meeting-centre generally.

22. *the doctors of the law.* The Greek word means literally scribes. In the gentile world scribes were simply skilled writers, or clerks of one sort or another. But among Jews the word generally meant someone who had had a special training in the interpretation and application of the Jewish Law, that is, the Books of Moses (Genesis to Deuteronomy) together with the great body of traditions that had grown up round them. Hence *doctors* (i.e. accredited teachers) *of the law* is a good rendering. These scribes tended to quote precedents: their strength lay not in originality but in wide knowledge of 'case-law'. Jesus, with no legal training, astonished his hearers by his independent authority.

24. *the Holy One of God.* A rarely used title. In the New Testament, it occurs, besides this place, only at Luke 4: 34, parallel to this passage, and at John 6: 69. In Ps. 16: 10 a

comparable phrase is used of one specially belonging to God. *

SIMON'S MOTHER-IN-LAW CURED, AND MANY OTHERS;
JESUS MOVES ON; A LEPER CURED;
THE PARALYSED MAN

On leaving the synagogue they went straight to the house 29 of Simon and Andrew; and James and John went with them. Simon's mother-in-law was ill in bed with fever. 30 They told him about her at once. He came forward, took 31 her by the hand, and helped her to her feet. The fever left her and she waited upon them.

That evening after sunset they brought to him all who 32 were ill or possessed by devils; and the whole town was 33 there, gathered at the door. He healed many who suffered 34 from various diseases, and drove out many devils. He would not let the devils speak, because they knew who he was.

Very early next morning he got up and went out. 35 He went away to a lonely spot and remained there in prayer. But Simon and his companions searched him 36 out, found him, and said, 'They are all looking for you.' 37 He answered, 'Let us move on to the country towns in 38 the neighbourhood; I have to proclaim my message there also; that is what I came out to do.' So all through Galilee 39 he went, preaching in the synagogues and casting out the devils.

Once he was approached by a leper, who knelt before 40 him begging his help. 'If only you will,' said the man, 'you can cleanse me.' In warm indignation Jesus stretched 41 out his hand, touched him, and said, 'Indeed I will; be

42 clean again.' The leprosy left him immediately, and he
43 was clean. Then he dismissed him with this stern warning:
44 'Be sure you say nothing to anybody. Go and show yourself to the priest, and make the offering laid down by
45 Moses for your cleansing; that will certify the cure.' But
the man went out and made the whole story public; he
spread it far and wide, until Jesus could no longer show
himself in any town, but stayed outside in the open
country. Even so, people kept coming to him from all
quarters.

2   When after some days he returned to Capernaum, the
2 news went round that he was at home; and such a crowd
collected that the space in front of the door was not big
enough to hold them. And while he was proclaiming the
3 message to them, a man was brought who was paralysed.
4 Four men were carrying him, but because of the crowd
they could not get him near. So they opened up the roof
over the place where Jesus was, and when they had broken
through they lowered the stretcher on which the paralysed
5 man was lying. When Jesus saw their faith, he said to the
paralysed man, 'My son, your sins are forgiven.'

6   Now there were some lawyers sitting there and they
7 thought to themselves, 'Why does the fellow talk like
that? This is blasphemy! Who but God alone can forgive
8 sins?' Jesus knew in his own mind that this was what they
were thinking, and said to them: 'Why do you harbour
9 thoughts like these? Is it easier to say to this paralysed
man, "Your sins are forgiven", or to say, "Stand up, take
10 your bed, and walk"? But to convince you that the Son
of Man has the right on earth to forgive sins'—he turned
11 to the paralysed man—'I say to you, stand up, take your

bed, and go home.' And he got up, and at once took his  12
stretcher and went out in full view of them all, so that
they were astounded and praised God. 'Never before',
they said, 'have we seen the like.'

 

✴ 32. *after sunset*, because the Jewish day was generally
measured from sunset to sunset, and only at sunset would the
Sabbath be ended. Sabbath (see note on verse 21) means
'cessation', and loyal Jews were under an obligation to cease
from work of any kind on this day (see Exod. 20: 10, etc.).
Almost stifled by the milling crowds while daylight lasts,
Jesus has to escape for quiet and leisured prayer by getting up
very early the next morning. Then he moves on to a widespread preaching campaign, refusing to be held down by his
huge success and popularity in any one locality.

38. *that is what I came out to do.* The parallel phrase in Luke
4: 43 interprets this as a theological statement about the divine
mission of Jesus: 'that is what I was sent to do'.

40–5. The words in Hebrew and Greek translated in the
Old and New Testaments by 'leprosy' appear not to indicate
the same disease as is generally known as leprosy today, but
other and less serious skin diseases (see Lev. 13 for a description).
It was one of the duties of the priests (see Lev. 13 again) to
pronounce when a man must be expelled from the community
as 'unclean', and when he might be received back again. This
was not exactly a medical matter of hygiene (see note on
7: 1–8); rather, it was held that certain conditions could make
the whole people religiously impure, and those who suffered
from them must therefore be excluded. If a man got well
enough to be received back again into the community, he had
to offer certain sacrifices (see Lev. 14). Jesus accepts these
Jewish laws, and, having cured the leper, he clinches it by
telling him to get his cure officially 'certified', as it were.

Why did Jesus urge him not to spread the story? Partly,
perhaps, because, if the crowds became even denser, Jesus

would be unable to give effective help to any individuals; and partly because he wanted his message to carry its own weight, without the publicity of spectacular stories. But the excited man could not keep his mouth shut.

2: 1. *at home.* Presumably in some house which Jesus had made his home—possibly Simon Peter's (see 1: 29).

5. *When Jesus saw their faith.* Sometimes one person's confidence in God's goodness can make it possible for another —some friend of his—to receive help. It was the faith of his four friends which helped this man. Seeing this, Jesus starts by telling the man that his sins are forgiven. We are not told why. It certainly does not follow that the New Testament represents all disease as the direct result of the sufferer's own sin. Indeed, John 9: 2-3 seems expressly to deny this: 'It is not that this man or his parents sinned....' Did Jesus intuitively see, perhaps, that the paralysis, in this particular case, was the psychological result of a sense of guilt?

At any rate, Jesus's declaration of forgiveness caused a scandal among the theologians. The *lawyers* (verse 6) are the same as the doctors of the law in 1: 22, that is, interpreters of the law. A fuller explanation of this will be found in the note on 1: 22. They may have been there expressly to spy on Jesus. He is already becoming suspect as a danger to the type of Judaism which depended on elaborate laws and regulations and which was more interested in authority than in persons.

They complained that a mere man had no authority to forgive sins. That was God's prerogative. Who was this man who blasphemously dared to usurp it? Jesus did not argue; he merely asked whether it was easier to assert something, like forgiveness, the reality of which could not be visibly tested, or something, like the cure of paralysis, which undoubtedly could be tested. Obviously the latter is the test case: if Jesus's word can cure the man, then who is to deny that he can also forgive him? Thus, the incident is a dramatic example of what was discussed above (pp. 15-16)—a visible deed of power being

22

a sign of victory over the Opposition at an invisible and even deeper level. Such victory is a sign that, in a unique sense, the sovereignty of God is identified with what Jesus does.

On *the Son of Man* (verse 10), see below (8: 27 — 9: 1). It is a special term used in relation to the mission and purpose of Jesus; but its particular relevance here, and at 2: 28 below, is less clear than in the later occurrence. *

### STORIES OF OPPOSITION: 2: 13 — 3: 6

#### THE CALL OF LEVI; FASTING; THE SABBATH

Once more he went away to the lake-side. All the crowd 13 came to him, and he taught them there. As he went along, 14 he saw Levi son of Alphaeus at his seat in the custom-house, and said to him, 'Follow me'; and Levi rose and followed him.

When Jesus was at table in his house, many bad characters—tax-gatherers and others—were seated with him and 15 his disciples; for there were many who followed him. Some doctors of the law who were Pharisees noticed him 16 eating in this bad company, and said to his disciples, 'He eats with tax-gatherers and sinners!' Jesus heard it and 17 said to them, 'It is not the healthy that need a doctor, but the sick; I did not come to invite virtuous people, but sinners.'

Once, when John's disciples and the Pharisees were 18 keeping a fast, some people came to him and said, 'Why is it that John's disciples and the disciples of the Pharisees are fasting, but yours are not?' Jesus said to them, 'Can 19 you expect the bridegroom's friends to fast while the bridegroom is with them? As long as they have the bridegroom with them, there can be no fasting. But the time 20 will come when the bridegroom will be taken away from them, and on that day they will fast.

21 'No one sews a patch of unshrunk cloth on to an old coat; if he does, the patch tears away from it, the new from
22 the old, and leaves a bigger hole. No one puts new wine into old wine-skins; if he does, the wine will burst the skins, and then wine and skins are both lost. Fresh skins for new wine!'

23 One Sabbath he was going through the cornfields; and his disciples, as they went, began to pluck ears of corn.
24 The Pharisees said to him, 'Look, why are they doing
25 what is forbidden on the Sabbath?' He answered, 'Have you never read what David did when he and his men were
26 hungry and had nothing to eat? He went into the House of God, in the time of Abiathar the High Priest, and ate the sacred bread, though no one but a priest is allowed to eat it, and even gave it to his men.'

27 He also said to them, 'The Sabbath was made for the
28 sake of man and not man for the Sabbath: therefore the Son of Man is sovereign even over the Sabbath.'

3 On another occasion when he went to synagogue, there was a man in the congregation who had a withered arm;
2 and they were watching to see whether Jesus would cure him on the Sabbath, so that they could bring a charge
3 against him. He said to the man with the withered arm,
4 'Come and stand out here.' Then he turned to them: 'Is it permitted to do good or to do evil on the Sabbath, to save
5 life or to kill?' They had nothing to say; and, looking round at them with anger and sorrow at their obstinate stupidity, he said to the man, 'Stretch out your arm.' He
6 stretched it out and his arm was restored. But the Phari-

sees, on leaving the synagogue, began plotting against him with the partisans of Herod to see how they could make away with him.

⁂ 14. *Levi son of Alphaeus.* In Matt. 9: 9 what is evidently the same incident gives the name as Matthew, not Levi. Mark 3: 18 mentions Matthew, but in that verse Alphaeus is the father, not of Matthew but of James. It is far from clear, therefore, whether Matthew and Levi can be alternative names for the same person. Neither can we be sure that tradition is right in associating that Matthew with the Gospel that now bears the name. We must be content not to know more about Levi than is here stated.

He was one of the hated class of tax-collectors—Jews who were paid by the Roman government to collect taxes for Rome from their fellow-Jews. Their unpatriotic trade was bad enough; but, in addition, they probably added as much as they could to their pay by extorting extra taxes, thus making themselves doubly detested. Round Levi was a set of people of the type most abhorred by the religious and patriotic Jews, *bad characters—tax-gatherers and others* (verse 15); and Jesus was criticized by some Pharisee-scribes for fraternizing with them.

16. For *doctors of the law*, see note on 1: 22. The Pharisees were specially devout Jews who tried to keep the Law of Moses in every detail. They were, in this respect, the successors of the martyr-loyalists who had suffered for their faith two centuries earlier, in the days of the brave patriot leaders known as the Maccabees or Hasmonaeans. These are alluded to, by two different words, both translated 'saints', in Dan. 7: 18 and in certain of the Psalms (e.g. 149: 9 N.E.B. 'faithful servants'), and described in the Apocrypha (see the Books of the Maccabees). The name, *Pharisees*, seems to have been interpreted to mean 'the separated ones', indicating their desire to be separate from contamination and sin; but it is possible that it really meant *exponents* of the Jewish Law; or, again, it has

been suggested that the name originally had something to do with certain of their beliefs being of *Persian* origin. They did hold certain beliefs not directly stated in the Books of Moses, such as that, for devout Jews, death would be followed ultimately by resurrection. Though with the very highest motives, they ran the risk of becoming self-righteous and priggish, and it is this that brought Jesus into such sharp conflict with them. Jesus's devastating reply to their criticisms (verse 17) implies that these virtuous critics are really just the people who need help, but who are too proud to accept it. Jesus was quick to recognize human need wherever it might be, but it was mostly the less respectable who were ready to accept his help: the others, including the professionally religious, were held back by pride and vested interests.

Just what Jesus called Levi to do, instead of his former occupation, is not clear—unless we do identify him with the Matthew of 3 : 18, in which case he became one of the Twelve, the intimate circle of Jesus's closest disciples who travelled about with him and shared his work (see note on 3 : 16).

18–22. Jesus had been criticized for the company he kept: here is a further ground for complaint—he did not observe the recognized forms of voluntary self-discipline like a religious specialist.

*John* is John the Baptist; for *the Pharisees*, see the preceding section. Abstaining from food was one of the recognized practices of Jewish piety; it was thought, at least by some, to be a means of winning God's pity or favour; it was also regarded as a good preparation for receiving divine revelations. Jesus declares that you cannot compel people to fast while they are celebrating a wedding. In other words, he compares himself and his friends to the most cheerful company imaginable.

It is possible that the allusion to a period of fasting which is to come *when the bridegroom* has been *taken away* may have been attached to the original words of Jesus at a later date, when the Christian Church had itself begun to adopt the practice. There is a definite reference to fasting on special days in the handbook of Church discipline called the *Didache* or Teaching of the Twelve Apostles, which comes from the early days of the Church. (See *Understanding the New Testament*, p. 107.) On the other hand, the reference to fasting may have been a genuine prediction by Jesus himself who foresaw that the present joy would one day be clouded by death and separation.

This saying is followed up, verses 21-2, by two vivid little parables, which seem to say that Jesus was introducing something so absolutely new and revolutionary that he could not be expected to try to accommodate it to the standard religious practices of the Jews. Can you imagine a housewife so stupid as to patch a rotten old garment with a piece of strong new cloth that still had to do its shrinking; or a man filling old leather wine-skins, which were wearing thin and had lost their capacity to stretch, with the fresh wine that had yet to do its fierce fermenting and expanding?

Two incidents follow illustrating further criticism from the religious experts: Jesus, they complain, is breaking the Sabbath-law, for which, see notes on 1: 21 and 32.

23-8. *the cornfields.* If religion is primarily a matter of rules, as it was for certain groups of Jews (for the Pharisees, see note on 2: 16), then it is necessary to define those rules exactly. It is not enough to say 'cease work on the Sabbath!' You have to define what constitutes work. This had led to rather ridiculous rules, such that it was possible to accuse Jesus's friends of breaking the Sabbath by performing with their hands what amounted to grinding corn.

Jesus's defence against this attack is two-fold: first, he appeals to an Old Testament precedent, to show that reputable people had, under the stress of need, broken a ritual law— David had eaten the special bread from a temple (see 1 Sam. 21: *Abiathar* in Mark seems to be a slip for Ahimelech there). Then he states a general principle underlying any such action: Was the Sabbath-law framed for its own sake? Of course not!

It was framed for the benefit of man, to give him time to worship God and to relax. One should always look for the purpose of a law, not treat it mechanically. But finally, Jesus adds the strange words: *therefore the Son of Man is sovereign even over the Sabbath.* This seems to go a step further still. Besides asserting that man in general is more important than the mere letter of the law, it asserts something, apparently, about Jesus in particular. On *the Son of Man*, see above (2: 10) and below (8: 27 — 9: 1).

3: 1–6. The man with a withered arm. Once again, the definition of 'work' on the Sabbath is at issue; and again Jesus goes back to first principles: Is the good principle that the Sabbath should be kept for worship and rest really meant to prevent so good a deed as healing the man forthwith? Jesus is grieved at the obstinate antagonism that prevents the religious experts from gladly accepting the point. His determination to put persons above mere things has earned him bitter enemies.

6. For *the Pharisees*, see note on 2: 16.

*the partisans of Herod* (see 8: 15) are thought to have been supporters of the dynasty of the Herods. Outside Judaea, which was under a sort of Roman viceroy called a prefect or procurator, Palestine was at this time governed by several Jewish or semi-Jewish princes, including members of the family of Herod. See note on 6: 14. ✻

VAST SUCCESS AND MANY CURES; THE TWELVE;
MISUNDERSTANDING ALL ROUND

7 Jesus went away to the lake-side with his disciples. Great
8 numbers from Galilee, Judaea and Jerusalem, Idumaea and Transjordan, and the neighbourhood of Tyre and Sidon,
9 heard what he was doing and came to see him. So he told his disciples to have a boat ready for him, to save him from
10 being crushed by the crowd. For he cured so many that sick people of all kinds came crowding in upon him to

touch him. The unclean spirits too, when they saw him, 11 would fall at his feet and cry aloud, 'You are the Son of God'; but he insisted that they should not make him 12 known.

He then went up into the hill-country and called the 13 men he wanted; and they went and joined him. He ap- 14 pointed twelve as his companions, whom he would send out to proclaim the Gospel, with a commission to drive 15 out devils. So he appointed the Twelve: to Simon he 16 gave the name Peter; then came the sons of Zebedee, 17 James and his brother John, to whom he gave the name Boanerges, Sons of Thunder; then Andrew and Philip and 18 Bartholomew and Matthew and Thomas and James the son of Alphaeus and Thaddaeus and Simon, a member of the Zealot party, and Judas Iscariot, the man who betrayed 19 him.

He entered a house; and once more such a crowd 20 collected round them that they had no chance to eat. When his family heard of this, they set out to take charge 21 of him; for people were saying that he was out of his mind.

The doctors of the law, too, who had come down from 22 Jerusalem, said, 'He is possessed by Beelzebub', and, 'He drives out devils by the prince of devils.' So he called 23 them to come forward, and spoke to them in parables: 'How can Satan drive out Satan? If a kingdom is divided 24 against itself, that kingdom cannot stand; if a household is 25 divided against itself, that house will never stand; and if 26 Satan is in rebellion against himself, he is divided and cannot stand; and that is the end of him.

'On the other hand, no one can break into a strong 27

man's house and make off with his goods unless he has first tied the strong man up; then he can ransack the house.

28 'I tell you this: no sin, no slander, is beyond forgiveness
29 for men; but whoever slanders the Holy Spirit can never
30 be forgiven; he is guilty of eternal sin.' He said this because they had declared that he was possessed by an unclean spirit.

31 Then his mother and his brothers arrived, and remaining outside sent in a message asking him to come out to them.
32 A crowd was sitting round and word was brought to him: 'Your mother and your brothers are outside asking for
33 you.' He replied, 'Who is my mother? Who are my
34 brothers?' And looking round at those who were sitting in the circle about him he said, 'Here are my mother and
35 my brothers. Whoever does the will of God is my brother, my sister, my mother.'

* 11. *the Son of God.* See note on 1: 9–13; and, for Jesus's recognition by 'the Opposition', see 1: 24.

For Jesus's care to avoid publicity, see note on 1: 40–5.

16. *The Twelve* is the term applied to the men called 'apostles', that is, special messengers, in the corresponding passage in Luke 6: 13 and in Mark 6: 30. Jesus seems to have had in mind the twelve tribes of Israel: he chooses a body of associates who will represent true Israel. If so, it is striking that he does not count himself. Does this imply that Jesus stands outside and above Israel? A tremendous claim seems here to be silently and unobtrusively made.

Very much could be said about these Twelve, but three things must be noted:

(i) Simon Peter comes to the head of the list, and his brother Andrew drops away to fourth place, separated by the other pair of fishermen brothers, James and John (see above,

1: 16–20). Peter is going to hold this place of leadership, in spite of conspicuous failures, right through to the period after the death and resurrection of Jesus: see Acts 1: 15.

(ii) It is interesting that one of the Twelve, another Simon, was (verse 18) *a member of the Zealot party*, if this is the right interpretation of the word *Zelotes*. The Zealots were extreme nationalists, who carried daggers and were prepared to adopt the tactics of underground revolutionaries to turn out the Romans. Jesus himself steadily refused to be manœuvred by the patriots into using violence: and it is evidence of his wide appeal and his readiness to take immense risks that he chose such a man as one of his intimates.

(iii) Jesus's acceptance of all the hazards that go with a joint enterprise reaches its climax in (verse 19) *Judas Iscariot* (meaning perhaps 'Judas the man from a place called Kerioth'), *the man who betrayed him* (see 14: 10–11).

We know little or nothing about the others; but it appears that Jesus chose what we might call an entirely layman's team, including four fishermen, an ex-tax-collector, if Matthew (verse 18) is indeed the same as Levi (see note on 2: 14 above), and a fanatical nationalist, but, so far as the evidence goes, no priests or theologians.

21. Jesus's own relations think he must be mad: instead of following his father's trade and settling down to an ordinary life, he is mixed up in these odd situations—seething crowds, spectacular cures, a very mixed assortment of intimates. So they try to rescue him (verses 21, 31–5). But Jesus resolutely follows God's call: his true relations, he says, are those who obey God. It must have been unspeakably costly to both him and his mother when he made this hard decision. It is clear that, according to Mark, Jesus's mother and brothers failed at this stage to understand him. But his resolute determination was justified: they understood afterwards, and Acts 1: 14 shows them, after the resurrection, assembled with the other disciples in Jerusalem.

Between the two parts of the account of this breach with

his family comes the slanderous accusation from the jealous theologians (verses 22–30). Yes, say these *doctors of the law* (see note on 1: 22), his cures are spectacular, but it is because he is in league with Beelzebub—an obscure name for, apparently, a demon-prince.

In reply, Jesus appeals to commonsense: it does not make sense for Satan to be fighting himself! No: it must be that here is someone strong enough to conquer Satan. And then comes the terrifying statement (verses 28–30) that such blind jealousy, which, seeing obvious good, deliberately calls this work of God's Spirit the work of Satan, is unforgivable. This is a hard saying, and difficult to understand. But two things, at least, have been well said about it:

(i) If a person is afraid that he has committed an unforgivable sin, his very concern shows that he has not: the essence of this sin is its callous blindness. Out of jealousy, it just refuses to recognize good, and, as long as it does this, it cannot accept forgiveness.

(ii) The ones who seem to be in greatest danger of it are not the lay people but the religious leaders, with their rivalries and self-regarding convictions.  ✻


PARABLES: 4: 1–34

✻ There was a time when it was thought that the Gospel parables were intended to carry a spiritual message in every single detail—a view which led to very fanciful and elaborate interpretations. But careful research into the actual circumstances of Jesus's life and work, and, still more, improved understanding of the way in which the traditions about his teaching were adapted and applied by early Christian teachers, have led to the recognition that, generally at any rate, Jesus told a parable in such a way as to make one or two points only. A parable was not an elaborate *allegory*, such that each detail is invented to suggest a spiritual counterpart, but a genuine *analogy*. Very often the analogy was drawn from living things such as seeds and plants. Jesus liked to draw a parallel between processes familiar to a rural society—farming and so forth— and the processes by which human character grows and develops: as with seed in a field, so with God's message among men. Or he would draw a parallel between the relation of man to man at one level and the relation of God to man at another: as with father and son, so with God and his worshipper.

This has led to the assumption that wherever, in the Gospels, a parable is applied as though it were a detailed allegory, this is due not to Jesus himself but to the early Christian teachers, who adapted and applied the original parables until they came to be written down with this later, allegorical application attached to them: the original parable had grown into an allegory in the process of transmission.

This is no doubt often true. The detailed allegorization of the parable of the weeds among the wheat in Matt. 13: 36-43 is a likely example. But it should not be assumed, without further testing, that this is necessarily and invariably the case. The application of the parable of the sower in the present chapter will be discussed when we come to it.

The method of teaching by parable was not invented by Jesus. The Old Testament contains some parables, as well as some allegories: a famous parable is the one told by the prophet Nathan to convince King David of his sin (2 Sam. 12: 1-7). The later Jewish writings, including those of the learned teachers, the rabbis, also contain illustrative stories of these types. But the extraordinary depth and penetration of the parables of the Gospels are, in the main, unrivalled, and set them in a class quite by themselves. *

### THE SOWER

On another occasion he began to teach by the lake-side. **4** The crowd that gathered round him was so large that he had to get into a boat on the lake, and there he sat, with the whole crowd on the beach right down to the water's edge.

2 And he taught them many things by parables.

As he taught he said:

3, 4 'Listen! A sower went out to sow. And it happened that as he sowed, some seed fell along the footpath; and the

5 birds came and ate it up. Some seed fell on rocky ground, where it had little soil, and it sprouted quickly because it

6 had no depth of earth; but when the sun rose the young corn was scorched, and as it had no root it withered

7 away. Some seed fell among thistles; and the thistles shot

8 up and choked the corn, and it yielded no crop. And some of the seed fell into good soil, where it came up and grew, and bore fruit; and the yield was thirtyfold, sixtyfold,

9 even a hundredfold.' He added, 'If you have ears to hear, then hear.'

10 When he was alone, the Twelve and others who were

11 round him questioned him about the parables. He replied, 'To you the secret of the kingdom of God has been given; but to those who are outside everything comes by way of

12 parables, so that (as Scripture says) they may look and look, but see nothing; they may hear and hear, but understand nothing; otherwise they might turn to God and be forgiven.'

13 So he said, 'You do not understand this parable? How

14 then are you to understand any parable? The sower sows

15 the word. Those along the footpath are people in whom the word is sown, but no sooner have they heard it than Satan comes and carries off the word which has been sown

16 in them. It is the same with those who receive the seed on rocky ground; as soon as they hear the word, they accept

17 it with joy, but it strikes no root in them; they have no

34

staying-power; then, when there is trouble or persecution on account of the word, they fall away at once. Others 18 again receive the seed among thistles; they hear the word, but worldly cares and the false glamour of wealth and all 19 kinds of evil desire come in and choke the word, and it proves barren. And there are those who receive the seed 20 in good soil; they hear the word and welcome it; and they bear fruit thirtyfold, sixtyfold, or a hundredfold.'

⁂ 8. *the yield was thirtyfold, sixtyfold, even a hundredfold*: meaning, perhaps, that, sown in the good ground, some single grains grew into plants of which some bore thirty grains each, some sixty, some a hundred.

9. *If you have ears to hear, then hear*: meaning 'Now think that one out for yourself, if you can!' See the next note.

10–12. This paragraph on the function of parables is perhaps meant, like verses 33–4 below, to describe what happened not just once, after the telling of this particular parable, but frequently. It was in private, afterwards, that the Twelve (see 3: 16) and others with them came for further instruction; and it was then that Jesus used to tell them that God's reign (see note on 1: 15) was a secret revealed only to those who, like them, had listened enough to come for more. It is, in fact, a comment on the phrase about hearing in verse 9. You can hear without making your own what you hear—without responding and acting on it; if so, you remain 'outside': you have got no further than simply hearing the parable; you have not begun to crack it open and get its kernel. Those who get no further are like the unresponsive people to whom the prophet Isaiah was sent (here Isa. 6: 9–10 is in part quoted): he was told, They will hear without hearing and see without seeing; otherwise—this is a bit of sarcasm, not meant to be taken in a solemnly literal way—they might actually repent! This passage is often interpreted as though it seriously meant that parables were *designed* to be obscure and to prevent response. If so, it is so far out of tune with Jesus's outlook that no doubt it would be correct to assume that it is an addition by the early Christians when they felt baffled by the unresponsiveness of the Jews. But why take it so literally, and with such prosaic solemnity? Does it not mean: 'You cannot teach people by spoon-feeding: you must set them a puzzle to think out for themselves; those who start to crack it are getting somewhere. There is no short-cut to understanding'?

13–20. If verses 10–12 describe what frequently happened, verses 13–20 now give a specific example of how Jesus interpreted a particular parable—this parable of the sower which we have just heard told. The interpretation makes it an allegory, in the sense defined in the note at the beginning of this chapter, although a simple and direct allegory. It takes each kind of soil and gives it a spiritual meaning. For this reason it is often treated as an application of the parable by the early church, not an application made by Jesus himself. But there is no evidence that Jesus never used allegory; and this is such a good and natural allegory, in which each point is itself a quite straightforward miniature parable, that Jesus himself may well have used it.

It means precisely what verses 11–12 have been interpreted to mean: the words may be sound and lively enough, but it is up to each hearer to let them sink in and become fruitful. If he only hears without responding—without doing something about it and committing himself to their meaning—then the words are in danger of being lost, or of never coming to anything. The whole story thus becomes a parable about the learner's responsibility, and about the importance of learning with one's whole will and obedience, and not merely with one's head.

If this application is rejected as a secondary addition, not originally given by Jesus himself, then the original parable of Jesus presumably meant: the results of preaching the Gospel are considerable, despite all hindrances and misadventures. But that seems rather a limited and feeble sense to get out of so detailed a story. ✳

### SAYINGS ABOUT UNDERSTANDING;
### THE SEED GROWS BY ITSELF; THE HARVEST WILL COME;
### THE MUSTARD SEED; CLOSING SUMMARY

He said to them, 'Do you bring in the lamp to put it under 21
the meal-tub, or under the bed? Surely it is brought to be
set on the lamp-stand. For nothing is hidden unless it is 22
to be disclosed, and nothing put under cover unless it is
to come into the open. If you have ears to hear, then 23
hear.'

He also said, 'Take note of what you hear; the measure 24
you give is the measure you will receive, with something
more besides. For the man who has will be given more, 25
and the man who has not will forfeit even what he has.'

He said, 'The kingdom of God is like this. A man 26
scatters seed on the land; he goes to bed at night and gets 27
up in the morning, and the seed sprouts and grows—how,
he does not know. The ground produces a crop by itself, 28
first the blade, then the ear, then full-grown corn in the
ear; but as soon as the crop is ripe, he plies the sickle, 29
because harvest-time has come.'

He said also, 'How shall we picture the kingdom of 30
God, or by what parable shall we describe it? It is like the 31
mustard-seed, which is smaller than any seed in the ground
at its sowing. But once sown, it springs up and grows 32
taller than any other plant, and forms branches so large
that the birds can settle in its shade.'

With many such parables he would give them his mes- 33
sage, so far as they were able to receive it. He never spoke 34
to them except in parables; but privately to his disciples
he explained everything.

* 21–5. These sayings, which may owe their present arrangement to Mark, come in different contexts scattered over Matthew and Luke (see, following Mark's order in each case, Matt. 5: 15; 10: 26; 7: 2; 25: 29; Luke 8: 16–18; 6: 38; 19: 26). As they are arranged here, they are perhaps meant to provide further comment on hearing and learning. Hearing is meant to lead to discovery: to hear without discovering is like lighting a lamp and then putting a cooking basin over it so that it goes out again! Further, to hear without responding with will and obedience is to lose what you hear—to gain nothing from it. Only the man who is ready himself to give—to give effort and willingness—will retain what he is given by others.

But it is impossible, without being sure of their original setting, to be certain what these sayings originally meant.

26–9. This little parable, which has no parallel in Matthew or Luke, seems to give the other side of the picture. The parable of the sower has emphasized the importance of receiving the 'seed' effectively—of responding. This parable of the ground which *produces a crop by itself* emphasizes the mysterious life-force in the seed. The most that the farmer can do is to sow it properly in suitable ground: he has to leave the seed itself and the good earth to do the rest. What did that mean? Did it mean what Paul meant when he wrote: 'I planted the seed, and Apollos watered it; but God made it grow. Thus it is not the gardeners with their planting and watering who count, but God, who makes it grow' (1 Cor. 3: 6–7)?

29. *but as soon as the crop is ripe.* This verse, on the other hand, seems to introduce a new point—the contrast between the inactive waiting and the activity of harvest when it comes. The kingdom of God will not be a secret for ever!

30–2. The parable of the mustard seed. The plant referred to is probably a *Sinapis* (formerly included in the genus *Brassica*); it has a small seed which grows quickly to a considerable height. *Sinapis arvensis* is the common charlock; table mustard is made from a mixture of the seeds of *S. alba* and *S. nigra*; the mustard seedlings of mustard and cress are those of *S. alba*.

God's reign (see notes on 1: 15) may seem small and insignificant in its beginnings; but it holds within it the most surprising forces. Matt. 13: 33 offers a parallel analogy from the almost invisible yeast which makes a big lump of dough rise.

33-4. A closing summary; see notes on 4: 10–12. ✶

# *Miracles of Christ*

✶ We have already had, in 1: 21 — 2: 12, accounts of several miracles. See the opening note on that section for remarks on the miraculous. But now Mark devotes a whole continuous section to this aspect of Jesus's work. ✶

### THE STORM; THE MADMAN

THAT DAY, in the evening, he said to them, 'Let us 35 cross over to the other side of the lake.' So they left 36 the crowd and took him with them in the boat where he had been sitting; and there were other boats accompanying him. A heavy squall came on and the waves broke over 37 the boat until it was all but swamped. Now he was in 38 the stern asleep on a cushion; they roused him and said, 'Master, we are sinking! Do you not care?' He awoke, 39 rebuked the wind, and said to the sea, 'Hush! Be still!' The wind dropped and there was a dead calm. He said to 40 them, 'Why are you such cowards? Have you no faith even now?' They were awestruck and said to one another, 41 'Who can this be? Even the wind and the sea obey him.'

5   So they came to the other side of the lake, into the
2  country of the Gerasenes. As he stepped ashore, a man
   possessed by an unclean spirit came up to him from among
3  the tombs where he had his dwelling. He could no longer
4  be controlled; even chains were useless; he had often been
   fettered and chained up, but he had snapped his chains and
   broken the fetters. No one was strong enough to master
5  him. And so, unceasingly, night and day, he would cry
   aloud among the tombs and on the hill-sides and cut him-
6  self with stones. When he saw Jesus in the distance, he ran
7  and flung himself down before him, shouting loudly,
   'What do you want with me, Jesus, son of the Most High
8  God? In God's name do not torment me.' (For Jesus was
   already saying to him, 'Out, unclean spirit, come out of
9  this man!') Jesus asked him, 'What is your name?' 'My
10 name is Legion,' he said, 'there are so many of us.' And
   he begged hard that Jesus would not send them out of the
   country.

11   Now there happened to be a large herd of pigs feeding
12 on the hill-side, and the spirits begged him, 'Send us
13 among the pigs and let us go into them.' He gave them
   leave; and the unclean spirits came out and went into the
   pigs; and the herd, of about two thousand, rushed over the
   edge into the lake and were drowned.

14   The men in charge of them took to their heels and
   carried the news to the town and country-side; and the
15 people came out to see what had happened. They came
   to Jesus and saw the madman who had been possessed by
   the legion of devils, sitting there clothed and in his
16 right mind; and they were afraid. The spectators told
   them how the madman had been cured and what had

happened to the pigs. Then they begged Jesus to leave the 17
district.

As he was stepping into the boat, the man who had been 18
possessed begged to go with him. Jesus would not allow
it, but said to him, 'Go home to your own folk and tell 19
them what the Lord in his mercy has done for you.'
The man went off and spread the news in the Ten Towns 20
of all that Jesus had done for him; and they were all
amazed.

\* 35–41. Modern readers find even the most startling accounts
of the cure of disease less hard to believe than this control over
the elements. We may believe comparatively easily that someone very great and good may, perhaps, so control persons' wills
as to make them well: but who can believe that the weather will
obey personal commands? If we believe in God as Creator,
and able, therefore, to manipulate the very particles out of
which this kind of situation is built up, we may, perhaps,
believe that he *can* control weather conditions; and, if Jesus is
God's perfect representative, the same may be said of him.
But it is another matter to believe that God *will* adjust the
weather to suit the needs of particular individuals. Our atti-
tude to that depends upon how far we think that this kind of
adjustment is in keeping with what we believe to be God's
settled purpose, namely, to treat persons as indeed persons
with free will and responsibility. In general, it seems more
like genuinely personal dealing if God helps persons to meet
danger and disaster outside their own selves and make something good out of them, than if he removes the difficulties so
as to make circumstances easy for them.

Whatever conclusion is reached about the story, the test
ought to be the consistency of God's character. It is right to
look for consistency. The mistake is to limit one's view to the
world treated as a merely mechanical system, and to ignore

the realm of personal relations, and—most important of all—God, as himself personal. The question is not so much: could this happen? as: would God do such a thing? It is difficult not to believe that the evangelist meant the story to be taken quite literally. But if it were not to be accepted literally, it would still be vigorous picture-language to describe Jesus as Master of the storms of life: of God it is said (Ps. 107: 29),

> The storm sank to a murmur,
> and the waves of the sea were stilled.

No wonder, then, that the disciples said: *Who can this be? Even the wind and the sea obey him.*

5: 1. *Gerasenes*. The Authorized Version follows a different reading, 'Gadarenes'. This is probably the best reading in the corresponding passage in Matthew (8: 28). In Luke 8: 26 the reading is less certain (N.E.B. 'Gergesenes', with marginal variants, Gerasenes and Gadarenes).

2. On so-called demon-possession, see the note on 1: 21–8. The particularly wild and savage madman described in this story felt as though he was occupied by a whole army of devils. Jesus accepts this diagnosis, and orders them out, and the man is restored to sanity.

11. The incident of the pigs raises unanswerable questions. Are we to explain the story away by saying that they were really stampeded by the man's wild cries? That is a lame explanation. Or is that bit of the story pure legend? If it is not, did Jesus really allow the owner to be robbed like this of a valuable herd of pigs? No doubt we all agree that the man's sanity was more valuable still: but the owner of the pigs was not consulted.

17. *they begged Jesus to leave the district* is a striking reaction, which, one would imagine, is unlikely to have been invented. If so, something had indeed happened which filled the local inhabitants with awe-stricken terror. But—

18–20. The cured man himself, in his gratitude and admiration, longs to stay with Jesus. Jesus, however, gives him

the harder task of staying at home and explaining there the
new life that he had been given.

20. *the Ten Towns* (Greek: *Decapolis*) constituted a league
of mainly gentile city-states situated, all except one, east or
south-east of the lake of Gennesaret, and modelled on the
Greek pattern of political life. It is natural enough that pigs,
whose flesh was forbidden to Jews (Lev. 11: 7, etc.), should
have been found in this gentile area.  ✳

### JAIRUS'S DAUGHTER; THE WOMAN SUFFERING
### FROM BLEEDING

As soon as Jesus had returned by boat to the other shore, 21
a great crowd once more gathered round him. While he
was by the lake-side, the president of one of the syna- 22
gogues came up, Jairus by name, and, when he saw him,
threw himself down at his feet and pleaded with him. 'My 23
little daughter', he said, 'is at death's door. I beg you to
come and lay your hands on her to cure her and save her
life.' So Jesus went with him, accompanied by a great 24
crowd which pressed upon him.

Among them was a woman who had suffered from 25
haemorrhages for twelve years; and in spite of long treat- 26
ment by many doctors, on which she had spent all she had,
there had been no improvement; on the contrary, she had
grown worse. She had heard what people were saying 27
about Jesus, so she came up from behind in the crowd and
touched his cloak; for she said to herself, 'If I touch even 28
his clothes, I shall be cured.' And there and then the source 29
of her haemorrhages dried up and she knew in herself that
she was cured of her trouble. At the same time Jesus, 30
aware that power had gone out of him, turned round in
the crowd and asked, 'Who touched my clothes?' His 31

disciples said to him, 'You see the crowd pressing upon
32 you and yet you ask, "Who touched me?"' Meanwhile
33 he was looking round to see who had done it. And the
woman, trembling with fear when she grasped what had
happened to her, came and fell at his feet and told him the
34 whole truth. He said to her, 'My daughter, your faith has
cured you. Go in peace, free for ever from this trouble.'
35    While he was still speaking, a message came from the
president's house, 'Your daughter is dead; why trouble the
36 Rabbi further?' But Jesus, overhearing the message as it
was delivered, said to the president of the synagogue, 'Do
37 not be afraid; only have faith.' After this he allowed no
one to accompany him except Peter and James and James's
38 brother John. They came to the president's house, where
he found a great commotion, with loud crying and
39 wailing. So he went in and said to them, 'Why this
crying and commotion? The child is not dead: she is
40 asleep'; and they only laughed at him. But after turning all
the others out, he took the child's father and mother and
his own companions and went in where the child was
41 lying. Then, taking hold of her hand, he said to her,
42 '*Talitha cum*', which means, 'Get up, my child.' Immediately the girl got up and walked about—she was
twelve years old. At that they were beside themselves
with amazement. He gave them strict orders to let no one
43 hear about it, and told them to give her something to eat.

✻ 22. *the president of one of the synagogues.* For synagogues, see
note on 1 : 21. The president of a synagogue was responsible for
organizing the worship and maintaining order.

25–34. The woman who stealthily touches Jesus's clothes

is cured, instantly; but not by some impersonal magic, for Jesus is somehow aware that he has given up healing energy for someone's benefit, and he insists on finding out who it is, and establishing personal contact. The woman, much alarmed at the publicity, owns up; and Jesus graciously reassures her, confirming her cure and telling her that it is her *faith* that has enabled her to receive it. Her faith was trust in Jesus; but it meant, ultimately, a trust in God, no doubt. The emphasis on faith (as in 2: 5 and 10: 52), and the establishment of personal contact between Jesus and the person healed, sharply distinguish a healing-story like this from stories of mere magic.

35-43. The story of Jairus's daughter, interrupted by the incident on the way to Jairus's house, is resumed. The girl is found to have died; but Jesus goes on; he tells the father that he must trust—*have faith*; he turns out the useless professional mourners, who were paid to wail and make a noise, and allows only the parents and his three close friends, Peter, James and John to enter the room where the dead child lies. Then he takes hold of her hand and speaks to her—the actual Aramaic used by Jesus is preserved: 'Talitha cum', '*Get up, my child*'. Quietly and practically he orders the astounded witnesses not to gossip about it, and directs that the girl be given some food.

The simplicity of this story, combined with its circumstantial detail, makes it exceedingly impressive. Some suggest, especially in view of Jesus's words, *The child is not dead: she is asleep*, that the girl was only in a coma. But it is perfectly clear that the evangelist understands it as a story of raising from death—sleep is just Jesus's word for death (as in John 11: 11-14); and it is difficult to see why a mere rousing from a coma—a condition perfectly well-known in those days—should ever have given rise to a miracle-story.

Raisings from death are described in the New Testament here (with parallel accounts in Matt. 9: 18-26; Luke 8: 40-56), in Luke 7: 11-17 (the widow's son), in John 11 (Lazarus), in Acts 9: 36-43 (Tabitha) and (perhaps) 20: 9-12 (Eutychus), and in two or three places in the Old Testament. In all these cases, it is assumed that the persons restored to life ultimately died again in the normal course of events. The resurrection of Jesus is different, for it is treated as a final and absolute raising into a new and eternal life. The mystery in both cases is profound—the more so because there is little or no satisfactory evidence for raisings from death in more recent times. But it is a hasty judgement merely to say that therefore they cannot have happened. *

## A PROPHET IN HIS OWN TOWN; THE MISSION OF THE TWELVE

**6** He left that place and went to his home town accompanied
**2** by his disciples. When the Sabbath came he began to teach in the synagogue; and the large congregation who heard him were amazed and said, 'Where does he get it from?', and, 'What wisdom is this that has been given him?',
**3** and, 'How does he work such miracles? Is not this the carpenter, the son of Mary, the brother of James and Joseph and Judas and Simon? And are not his sisters here
**4** with us?' So they fell foul of him. Jesus said to them, 'A prophet will always be held in honour except in his
**5** home town, and among his kinsmen and family.' He could work no miracle there, except that he put his hands
**6** on a few sick people and healed them; and he was taken aback by their want of faith.

**7** On one of his teaching journeys round the villages he summoned the Twelve and sent them out in pairs on a
**8** mission. He gave them authority over unclean spirits, and instructed them to take nothing for the journey beyond a
**9** stick: no bread, no pack, no money in their belts. They
**10** might wear sandals, but not a second coat. 'When you are admitted to a house', he added, 'stay there until you leave

those parts. At any place where they will not receive you 11
or listen to you, shake the dust off your feet as you leave,
as a warning to them.' So they set out and called publicly 12
for repentance. They drove out many devils, and many 13
sick people they anointed with oil and cured.

✻ 1–6. This section underlines the importance of faith (see
note on 5: 25–34), and represents Jesus as gravely hampered
by the jealous scepticism of his own family and townspeople.
See note on 3: 21 above.

3. *the carpenter*. This is the best evidence of Jesus's original
trade, though an alternative reading, *the carpenter's son*, may
be correct.

5. *He could work no miracle there, except*...is a very frank
admission of this dependence of Jesus on the response of those
whom he wished to help. (See the last paragraph but one of
the note on 1: 21 — 2: 12, p. 16.) In this case, the difficulty
seems to have been not failure to believe that Jesus could do
these things (see verse 2), but sheer jealousy and antagonism
and refusal to co-operate. Contrast the modified form in
Matt. 13: 58: 'he did not work many miracles there'.

7–13. Jesus's own work of preaching and healing is now
extended through his close friends and representatives, the
Twelve (see 3: 13–19). They are sent on a tour in pairs,
wearing only what they stand up in, so that they are bound to
rely on the hospitality of those to whom they are sent. This
became one of the recognized principles in the Church's
pastoral work. The saying 'the worker earns his keep', which
occurs in Matthew's version of this passage (Matt. 10: 10) and
in Luke's account of another mission—the mission of the
seventy-two (Luke 10: 7)—is repeated in 1 Tim. 5: 18. So,
too, in Acts 16: 15, Paul and his companions accept an in-
vitation from the woman named Lydia at Philippi to stay in
her house while they are evangelizing in the town. In 1 Cor. 9
and 2 Cor. 12: 13 ff., Paul admits that, in special circumstances,

he kept himself independent: but he has to defend his action. He did it because he was evidently being accused of making money out of the Gospel, and therefore had to avoid giving any handle for his critics. In general, the Christian principle is not proud independence, but a willingness to accept the risk and obligations of mutual dependence.

7, 12, 13. Jesus clearly expected his friends not only to call for a change of morals, but also to cure diseases, as he himself did. For *unclean spirits* see notes on 1: 21–8 and 5: 2. ✳

## THE DEATH OF JOHN THE BAPTIST

14 Now King Herod heard of it, for the fame of Jesus had spread; and people were saying, 'John the Baptist has been raised to life, and that is why these miraculous

15 powers are at work in him.' Others said, 'It is Elijah.' Others again, 'He is a prophet like one of the old prophets.'

16 But Herod, when he heard of it, said, 'This is John, whom I beheaded, raised from the dead.'

17 For this same Herod had sent and arrested John and put him in prison on account of his brother Philip's wife,

18 Herodias, whom he had married. John had told Herod,

19 'You have no right to your brother's wife.' Thus Herodias nursed a grudge against him and would willingly have

20 killed him, but she could not; for Herod went in awe of John, knowing him to be a good and holy man; so he kept him in custody. He liked to listen to him, although the listening left him greatly perplexed.

21 Herodias found her opportunity when Herod on his birthday gave a banquet to his chief officials and com-

22 manders and the leading men of Galilee. Her daughter came in and danced, and so delighted Herod and his guests that the king said to the girl, 'Ask what you like and I will

give it you.' And he swore an oath to her: 'Whatever you 23
ask I will give you, up to half my kingdom.' She went 24
out and said to her mother, 'What shall I ask for?' She
replied, 'The head of John the Baptist.' The girl hastened 25
back at once to the king with her request: 'I want you to
give me here and now, on a dish, the head of John the
Baptist.' The king was greatly distressed, but out of regard 26
for his oath and for his guests he could not bring himself
to refuse her. So the king sent a soldier of the guard with 27
orders to bring John's head. The soldier went off and
beheaded him in the prison, brought the head on a dish, 28
and gave it to the girl; and she gave it to her mother.

When John's disciples heard the news, they came and 29
took his body away and laid it in a tomb.


✴ For John the Baptist, see notes on 1: 1–8.

14. *King Herod*, that is, Herod Antipas. He was the son of
Herod the Great, the Jewish, or virtually Jewish, king who
figures in the story of the astrologers and the massacre of the
babies in Matt. 2. From the death of Herod the Great in 4 B.C.
until A.D. 39, Herod Antipas was king, by appointment of the
Roman Emperor Augustus, of the territory of Galilee and
Peraea, stretching from north-west to south-east of the Jordan
(see p. x). See Luke 3: 1 for the division of territories between
the various rulers.

Mark's account of John the Baptist's martyrdom is a 'flash-
back'. Herod, hearing marvellous stories about Jesus, imagines
that it must be John, returned from the grave with supernatural
powers to torment his guilty conscience; for Herod—as Mark
then goes on to describe—had executed him. As was noted on
1: 1–8, the Jewish historian Josephus attributes this action to
Herod's fear that John might prove to be a dangerous nationalist
revolutionary. Mark attributes it to the spite of *his brother*

*Philip's wife, Herodias* (verse 17). According to Josephus, she was the wife not of Philip but of a half-brother of Antipas's named Herod; but in any case Antipas's offence remains: he had divorced his first wife to marry her, and the Baptist, having had the courage to rebuke him for it, paid for it with his head. ✻

### A HUNGRY CROWD FED; THE SEQUEL; CLOSING SUMMARY

30 The apostles now rejoined Jesus and reported to him all
31 that they had done and taught. He said to them, 'Come with me, by yourselves, to some lonely place where you can rest quietly.' (For they had no leisure even to eat, so
32 many were coming and going.) Accordingly, they set off
33 privately by boat for a lonely place. But many saw them leave and recognized them, and came round by land, hurrying from all the towns towards the place, and arrived
34 there first. When he came ashore, he saw a great crowd; and his heart went out to them, because they were like sheep without a shepherd; and he had much to teach them.
35 As the day wore on, his disciples came up to him and said,
36 'This is a lonely place and it is getting very late; send the people off to the farms and villages round about, to buy
37 themselves something to eat.' 'Give them something to eat yourselves', he answered. They replied, 'Are we to go and spend twenty pounds on bread to give them a meal?'
38 'How many loaves have you?' he asked; 'go and see.' They found out and told him, 'Five, and two fishes also.'
39 He ordered them to make the people sit down in groups
40 on the green grass, and they sat down in rows, a hundred
41 rows of fifty each. Then, taking the five loaves and the two fishes, he looked up to heaven, said the blessing, broke the

loaves, and gave them to the disciples to distribute. He
also divided the two fishes among them. They all ate to 42
their hearts' content; and twelve great basketfuls of scraps 43
were picked up, with what was left of the fish. Those who 44
ate the loaves numbered five thousand men.

As soon as it was over he made his disciples embark and 45
cross to Bethsaida ahead of him, while he himself sent the
people away. After taking leave of them, he went up the 46
hill-side to pray. It grew late and the boat was already well 47
out on the water, while he was alone on the land. Some- 48
where between three and six in the morning, seeing them
labouring at the oars against a head-wind, he came towards
them, walking on the lake. He was going to pass them by;
but when they saw him walking on the lake, they thought 49
it was a ghost and cried out; for they all saw him and were 50
terrified. But at once he spoke to them: 'Take heart! It is
I; do not be afraid.' Then he climbed into the boat beside 51
them, and the wind dropped. At this they were completely dumbfounded, for they had not understood the 52
incident of the loaves; their minds were closed.

So they finished the crossing and came to land at Gen- 53
nesaret, where they made fast. When they came ashore, he 54
was immediately recognized; and the people scoured that 55
whole country-side and brought the sick on stretchers to
any place where he was reported to be. Wherever he went, 56
to farmsteads, villages, or towns, they laid out the sick in
the market-places and begged him to let them simply
touch the edge of his cloak; and all who touched him
were cured.

✻ 30–44. This, with its sequel, the walking on the water, is the only miracle-story, apart from the resurrection-stories, which all four Gospels include. Attempts have been made to explain it away as only an exaggerated account of how the immense crowd, seeing the minute picnic lunch of loaves and fishes gallantly produced, followed suit and brought out the food they had hitherto concealed and been unwilling to share! If this had really been the case, it would not have been remarkable enough even to give rise to an exaggerated and miraculous account. Alternatively, it is easy enough to say that it is not meant to be taken literally, but is a symbolical picture of the way in which Christ feeds the souls of men by his own self-sacrifice; and it is certainly likely enough that the Eucharist or Holy Communion, at which bread is distributed in the name of Christ with thanksgiving, was in the evangelist's mind as he wrote. But there is little or no evidence for the invention, out of nothing, of such symbolical stories at this stage in the Church's development; and it may be that the reader ought to grapple with it on its own terms as a miracle-story. In that case, he must reach his own conclusions, remembering to ask not so much: could this happen? as: would God do such a thing? (See the notes on 1: 21 — 2: 12 and 4: 35 — 5: 20.)

30. The apostles: see note on 3: 16.

45–52. It has been suggested that the vast concourse of men described in the preceding paragraph was not a chance crowd, but the beginnings of a nationalist rebellion. John's account (John 6: 15) says in so many words that they meant to come and seize Jesus to proclaim him king. If so, verse 45 hints that Jesus used masterly firmness. Sending his disciples ahead, out of harm's way, he sent the people away. He himself then withdrew up the hill-side to pray alone.

It is after this, towards daybreak, that he miraculously walks on the waters of the lake, rejoins his astonished and terrified friends, and causes the stiff wind to drop. Once again, the reader must ask: is this the Christians' way of expressing, in picture-language, their faith in Christ's almighty power? Is it

a legend that grew up round some perfectly normal incident?
Or did something utterly extraordinary really happen? In any
case—and most important of all—what does it mean? See the
last paragraph of the notes on 1: 21 — 2: 12 (p. 16).

53–6. A closing summary mentioning many healings.
*Simply touch the edge of his cloak*: compare 5: 25–34. *

# Growing Tension

* Hitherto the general impression has been of vast crowds,
great popularity, unhindered activity. Only occasionally has
the note of antagonism or jealousy been heard. But now comes
a section of conflict. Jesus is disappointing the hopes of those
who saw in him a potential leader of a nationalist rebellion. At
the same time, he is scandalizing the orthodox religious leaders.
In the resulting tension, Mark lets us begin to hear the sinister
note of murderous hatred. In this section of the Gospel, Jesus
is sometimes in conflict with opponents, sometimes engaged
on consolidating and training his inner circle for what is
coming. *

### RITUAL CLEANNESS; THE CORBAN LAW;
### THE REAL SOURCE OF DEFILEMENT

A GROUP of Pharisees, with some doctors of the law 7
who had come from Jerusalem, met him and noticed 2
that some of his disciples were eating their food with
'defiled' hands—in other words, without washing them.
(For the Pharisees and the Jews in general never eat with- 3
out washing the hands, in obedience to an old-established
tradition; and on coming from the market-place they 4
never eat without first washing. And there are many other

points on which they have a traditional rule to maintain, for example, washing of cups and jugs and copper bowls.)

5 Accordingly, these Pharisees and the lawyers asked him, 'Why do your disciples not conform to the ancient
6 tradition, but eat their food with defiled hands?' He answered, 'Isaiah was right when he prophesied about you hypocrites in these words: "This people pays me
7 lip-service, but their heart is far from me: their worship of me is in vain, for they teach as doctrines the command-
8 ments of men." You neglect the commandment of God, in order to maintain the tradition of men.'

9     He also said to them, 'How well you set aside the commandment of God in order to maintain your tradition!
10 Moses said, "Honour your father and your mother", and, "The man who curses his father or mother must suffer
11 death." But you hold that if a man says to his father or mother, "Anything of mine which might have been used for your benefit is Corban"' (meaning, set apart for God),
12 'he is no longer permitted to do anything for his father or
13 mother. Thus by your own tradition, handed down among you, you make God's word null and void. And many other things that you do are just like that.'

14     On another occasion he called the people and said to them, 'Listen to me, all of you, and understand this:
15 nothing that goes into a man from outside can defile him; no, it is the things that come out of him that defile a man.'

17     When he had left the people and gone indoors, his
18 disciples questioned him about the parable. He said to them, 'Are you as dull as the rest? Do you not see that nothing that goes from outside into a man can defile him,
19 because it does not enter into his heart but into his stomach,

and so passes out into the drain?' Thus he declared all
foods clean. He went on, 'It is what comes out of a man 20
that defiles him. For from inside, out of a man's heart, 21
come evil thoughts, acts of fornication, of theft, murder,
adultery, ruthless greed, and malice; fraud, indecency, 22
envy, slander, arrogance, and folly; these evil things all 23
come from inside, and they defile the man.'

✴ 1-8. The customs referred to here are not particularly
concerned with hygiene (see note on 1: 40-5). Unwashed
hands were criticized, not because of germs (of which nothing
was known), but because the specially careful Pharisees were,
by this time, beginning to make binding upon themselves the
ritual washings prescribed in Lev. 22: 6 for priests (see also
15: 13). For *Pharisees*, see note on 2: 16; for *doctors of the law*,
note on 1: 22. *Lawyers* in verse 5 renders the same word.

6. Jesus's reply to the complaint against his neglect of this
ritual detail is, in the words of Isa. 29: 13, that externals are
worse than useless unless the heart is in the right place. The
elaborate regulations—the tradition of men—which ministered
to the self-satisfaction of those who observed them, had
smothered the very purpose for which God's law had been
designed, namely, the glad and humble worship of God by
man.

9-13. Jesus proceeds to produce an example of the subtle
arguments (casuistry) by which the teachers of the Jewish Law
got round the humanity and true religion which the law was
originally meant to protect, and turned it topsy turvy. *Corban*
(verse 11) is just a Jewish word for something brought near to
God in worship—a sacrifice or dedicated offering. Apparently
the elaborations of the law were being applied so rigorously
that a dedication made hastily or in anger could not be revoked
even for the humane purpose of releasing money to support
needy parents; or it may even be that hard-hearted and

grasping men, by declaring some money or property *corban*, that is, dedicated to God, escaped the duty of helping their parents with it, and yet somehow kept it available for their own use.

14–23. Jesus sums up the whole situation by saying that what defiles a person is not what enters him but what comes out of him.

16. This verse, *If you have ears to hear, then hear*, is omitted because it is not found in all the manuscripts, and is probably not what Mark wrote here, whereas at 4: 9 it is probably correct.

17. Jesus's epigram is here called a *parable*. This word strictly means an analogy of some sort, and we have seen in chapter 4 (see notes there) the characteristics of the parables of Jesus. But the Greek word *parabole* is used to render a Jewish word which can also mean a riddle or epigram; and this is evidently the sense here. The disciples find it a difficult riddle, and ask for its meaning.

Jesus explains that by the epigram he meant that a person is not defiled by breaking a Jewish food-law and eating what the Jews regarded as ritually forbidden (e.g. pork). In saying this he opposed those Jews who made an unalterable principle of food-laws; he *declared all foods clean* (verse 19), in the sense that no foodstuff can, in itself, defile. Rather, what defiles is a foul imagination; for (verse 21) it is *out of a man's heart* that there *come evil thoughts*. . . . It has been well said that nothing is more potent for good or evil in a person's character than his imagination—what he dwells on in his private thoughts. ✳

### THE GENTILE WOMAN; THE MAN WHO WAS DEAF AND HAD A SPEECH IMPEDIMENT

24 Then he left that place and went away into the territory of Tyre. He found a house to stay in, and he would have liked to remain unrecognized, but this was impossible.

25 Almost at once a woman whose young daughter was

possessed by an unclean spirit heard of him, came in, and
fell at his feet. (She was a Gentile, a Phoenician of Syria 26
by nationality.) She begged him to drive the spirit out of
her daughter. He said to her, 'Let the children be satisfied 27
first; it is not fair to take the children's bread and throw it
to the dogs.' 'Sir,' she answered, 'even the dogs under the 28
table eat the children's scraps.' He said to her, 'For saying 29
that, you may go home content; the unclean spirit has
gone out of your daughter.' And when she returned 30
home, she found the child lying in bed; the spirit had
left her.

On his return journey from Tyrian territory he went 31
by way of Sidon to the Sea of Galilee through the territory
of the Ten Towns. They brought to him a man who was 32
deaf and had an impediment in his speech, with the request
that he would lay his hand on him. He took the man aside, 33
away from the crowd, put his fingers into his ears, spat,
and touched his tongue. Then, looking up to heaven, he 34
sighed, and said to him, '*Ephphatha*', which means 'Be
opened.' With that his ears were opened, and at the same 35
time the impediment was removed and he spoke plainly.
Jesus forbade them to tell anyone; but the more he forbade 36
them, the more they published it. Their astonishment 37
knew no bounds: 'All that he does, he does well,' they
said; 'he even makes the deaf hear and the dumb speak.'

* 24–30. Jesus withdraws to the far north—whether to escape
arrest or to escape the crowds and undesirable publicity (see last
paragraph of note on 1: 40–5) is not stated. In any case he cannot escape the importuning of the needy. The woman is not a
Jew, and Jesus's reply to her request implies that his ministry
is confined to the Jews: in the parallel passage, indeed, in

Matt. 15: 24, this is quite clear. But she cleverly parries his remarks and persists. Jesus yields, and the cure is worked.

Are we really to believe that Jesus was reluctant to give any help outside the Jewish people? Is not this a contradiction of such daring sayings as Matt. 8: 11-12, 'Many, I tell you, will come from east and west to feast with Abraham, Isaac, and Jacob in the kingdom of Heaven. But those who were born to the kingdom will be driven out into the dark...'? And, in any case, can we imagine Jesus refusing anyone in need? Perhaps the answer is that, whatever Jesus foresaw as the ultimate result of his mission, he deliberately concentrated, in his lifetime, on the Jews alone. Perhaps, too, something depends upon the tone of voice in which he made the protest and the look in his eye at the time. As soon as the Gentile woman rises to the situation, he is instantly ready to help.

31. Jesus's return route is strangely described and not easy to plot on a map (see p. x). Was the writer unfamiliar with the territory? For *the Ten Towns*, see note on 5: 20.

32-7. This healing-story contains no reference to faith on the part of the healed man. In the introductory notes to 1: 21 — 2: 12 it is emphasized that faith is generally an important factor in the healings by Jesus. But this man was deaf and partly dumb; it was natural that Jesus should have appealed to him not by words but by signs. He put his fingers into his deaf ears, and touched his tongue with spittle from his own mouth, as much as to say, 'Here, and here, I am ready to help you and calling upon you to respond.' Then he looks up as though to recall the presence of God, sighs, and, in his native Aramaic, commands the blocked organs to 'be opened'.

34. *he sighed* is a detail occurring in no other healing-story in the Gospels, and it has been compared with references to sighing or groaning in ancient magical practice. But it is quite natural here to interpret it as the sign of a deep and exhausting prayer—a yearning towards God on behalf of the helpless man. (It is perhaps different with 8: 12.)

37. The inner meaning of the story is underlined by a clever

hint. The phrase *had an impediment in his speech* (verse 32) represents a single Greek word, *mogilalos*. It is a far from common word, and its only occurrence in the ordinary Greek version of the Old Testament is at Isa. 35: 6. Here there is a poetical description of the fine things that will happen when God comes to help his people: 'Then shall blind men's eyes be opened, and the ears of the deaf unstopped. Then shall the lame man leap like a deer, and the tongue of the dumb [*mogilalos*] shout aloud' (Isa. 35: 5–6). So, Mark's choice of a word from this description of the new age seems to say to the reader, as Jesus might have said: 'If you have ears to hear, then hear.' *

ANOTHER HUNGRY CROWD FED;
THE PHARISEES DEMAND A SIGN

There was another occasion about this time when a huge **8** crowd had collected, and, as they had no food, Jesus called his disciples and said to them, 'I feel sorry for all these **2** people; they have been with me now for three days and have nothing to eat. If I send them home unfed, they will **3** turn faint on the way; some of them have come from a distance.' The disciples answered, 'How can anyone pro- **4** vide all these people with bread in this lonely place?' 'How many loaves have you?' he asked; and they **5** answered, 'Seven.' So he ordered the people to sit down **6** on the ground; then he took the seven loaves, and, after giving thanks to God, he broke the bread and gave it to his disciples to distribute; and they served it out to the people. They had also a few small fishes, which he blessed **7** and ordered them to distribute. They all ate to their **8** hearts' content, and seven baskets were filled with the scraps that were left. The people numbered about four **9** thousand. Then he dismissed them; and, without delay, **10** got into the boat with his disciples and went to the district of Dalmanutha.

11 Then the Pharisees came out and engaged him in discussion. To test him they asked him for a sign from heaven.
12 He sighed deeply to himself and said, 'Why does this generation ask for a sign? I tell you this: no sign shall be
13 given to this generation.' With that he left them, re-embarked, and went off to the other side of the lake.

---

\* 1–10. Another account, like that in 6: 30–44 (see notes there), of the miraculous feeding of a huge crowd: this time it is four thousand. It has been suggested that this is simply an alternative version of the same story, and that Mark has deliberately included both versions for symbolical purposes, the former representing the spiritual feeding of the Jews with the Gospel, the latter that of the Gentiles.

But it is difficult to detect any such intention, and it is impossible to prove even that the two stories spring from one and the same root: there are a number of differences in detail. One thing is clear, and that is that the evangelist himself intended to convey the impression of two distinct incidents, for in 8: 19–20 they are both expressly mentioned. Matthew also has the two stories, but Luke and John only the one.

11. For *the Pharisees* see note on 2: 16. The demand for demonstrative proof of divine authority was something which Jesus had had to resist for himself, according to the accounts of his testing in Matt. 4: 7, Luke 4: 12. It is true that, many times already, Mark has related the most startling signs of God's power and presence—the miracles, as we call them (see notes on 1: 21 — 2: 12). What Jesus resists, however, is the demand for such signs for their own sake, as though they could be in themselves guarantees, such as might be observed from outside by a neutral spectator. The claims of God can be known only by committing oneself in loyalty to him, not by standing

outside and arrogantly saying, 'Produce your evidence!'
John's Gospel is full of this contrast between the demand for
mere external proof, without surrendering one's security, and
the revelation which comes only when a man means business
and is prepared to take risks: 'Whoever has the will to do the
will of God shall know whether my teaching comes from
him...' (John 7:17). No wonder Jesus *sighed deeply* (verse 12)!
It is a difficult and demanding thing to find the right kind of
assurance, and the Pharisees were asking for it cheaply and on
their own terms. ✷

#### SLOW TO TAKE A HINT; A BLIND MAN CURED

Now they had forgotten to take bread with them; they 14
had no more than one loaf in the boat. He began to warn 15
them: 'Beware,' he said, 'be on your guard against the
leaven of the Pharisees and the leaven of Herod.' They 16
said among themselves, 'It is because we have no bread.'
Knowing what was in their minds, he asked them, 'Why 17
do you talk about having no bread? Have you no inkling
yet? Do you still not understand? Are your minds
closed? You have eyes: can you not see? You have ears: 18
can you not hear? Have you forgotten? When I broke 19
the five loaves among five thousand, how many basketfuls
of scraps did you pick up?' 'Twelve', they said. 'And 20
how many when I broke the seven loaves among four
thousand?' They answered, 'Seven.' He said, 'Do you 21
still not understand?'

They arrived at Bethsaida. There the people brought a 22
blind man to Jesus and begged him to touch him. He took 23
the blind man by the hand and led him away out of the
village. Then he spat on his eyes, laid his hands upon him,
and asked whether he could see anything. The man's sight 24

began to come back, and he said, 'I see men; they look like
25 trees, but they are walking about.' Jesus laid his hands on
his eyes again; he looked hard, and now he was cured so
26 that he saw everything clearly. Then Jesus sent him home,
saying, 'Do not tell anyone in the village.'

* 14. *they*: evidently the disciples.

15. *leaven*. It was usual in those days to make the bread
rise by adding some yeast or a piece of fermenting dough from
a previous baking. It is this ingredient that is called leaven;
and leaven had become a proverbial expression for something
which, though itself almost invisible, produced spectacular
results. In the parable of the yeast (Matt. 13: 33; Luke 13:
20–1, not in Mark—see note on 4: 30–2) it stands for something
good—the kingship of God as it secretly penetrates and per-
meates life; but here, and indeed generally in the Bible, it
stands for evil influence. *The leaven of the Pharisees* (see 2: 16)
probably means the kind of thing illustrated in the preceding
paragraph—their legalistic demands which made them miss
the heart of religion, which is joyful acceptance of personal
fellowship with God. *The leaven of Herod* possibly meant
Jewish nationalist intrigues: see notes on 3: 6 and 6: 14.

The disciples solemnly take Jesus's proverbial words literally,
thinking, since they have forgotten to bring sandwiches, that
they are being warned against accepting poisoned food from
others. Jesus replies that they are no better than the 'outsiders'
of 4: 11–12, who will not use their eyes or ears; have they so
soon forgotten that, with Jesus, they should never be anxious
about physical sustenance? For the two feedings of multitudes,
see note on 8: 1–13.

22–6. This miracle-story is particularly interesting as the
only one in the Gospels describing a gradual cure, in two stages.
The man's sight begins to come back, but imperfectly. It is
only after the second touch from Jesus that the cure is complete.
This is not an obvious pattern for a miracle-story to follow, if

it were being merely invented out of the imagination. As with the deaf and partly dumb man of 7: 31–7, so here, Jesus uses spittle: so with the blind man in John 9: 6. For another story about sight for the blind, see 10: 46–52.

If the arrangement of Mark's Gospel is deliberately designed to carry a message, it may be part of the design that we find, one after another, (i) a reference to the dullness of the disciples' minds (8: 18), (ii) the gradual opening of a man's eyes (this section), (iii) a partial and imperfect insight on the part of Peter (the next section), and (iv) the wonderful revelation granted to the three disciples at the transfiguration (9: 2–8). *

### PETER CALLS JESUS MESSIAH; THE CALL TO FACE DEATH; A SAYING ABOUT THE COMING OF THE KINGDOM

Jesus and his disciples set out for the villages of Caesarea 27 Philippi. On the way he asked his disciples, 'Who do men say I am?' They answered, 'Some say John the 28 Baptist, others Elijah, others one of the prophets.' 'And 29 you,' he asked, 'who do you say I am?' Peter replied: 'You are the Messiah.' Then he gave them strict orders 30 not to tell anyone about him; and he began to teach them 31 that the Son of Man had to undergo great sufferings, and to be rejected by the elders, chief priests, and doctors of the law; to be put to death, and to rise again three days afterwards. He spoke about it plainly. At this Peter took 32 him by the arm and began to rebuke him. But Jesus 33 turned round, and, looking at his disciples, rebuked Peter. 'Away with you, Satan,' he said; 'you think as men think, not as God thinks.'

Then he called the people to him, as well as his disciples, 34 and said to them, 'Anyone who wishes to be a follower of mine must leave self behind; he must take up his cross, and

35 come with me. Whoever cares for his own safety is lost;
but if a man will let himself be lost for my sake and for the
36 Gospel, that man is safe. What does a man gain by winning
37 the whole world at the cost of his true self? What can he
38 give to buy that self back? If anyone is ashamed of me
and mine in this wicked and godless age, the Son of Man
will be ashamed of him, when he comes in the glory of his
Father and of the holy angels.'

**9**     He also said, 'I tell you this: there are some of those
standing here who will not taste death before they have
seen the kingdom of God already come in power.'

\* By this time there are all sorts of speculations about who
Jesus can be. He is so obviously great, and also so mysterious that
some are asking themselves (like Herod Antipas, see note on
6: 14) whether he is John the Baptist restored to life. Others
are saying that the great Old Testament prophet Elijah, or one
of the other great prophets of the past, has returned to life.
'*And you,*' he asked, '*who do you say I am?*' (verse 29). Jesus and
his disciples—for some reason not stated—are once again
(compare 7: 24–30) travelling away from Jewish surroundings.
This time it is right up to the north-east of Palestine beyond
Galilee among the villages belonging to the city-state of
Caesarea Philippi, very near to the slopes of snow-capped
Mount Hermon. Here is an opportunity for Jesus to bring his
friends to grips with this mysterious question: Who is he?
What is his mission?

Peter is the one who seems generally to have found words—
not always wise or suitable words, but words, anyway. *You
are the Messiah* (verse 31). He has said it! Perhaps it was in
the minds of them all, but they were too timid to admit it.
Jesus must be the Messiah; but only Peter dared to admit it.

In the note on 1: 15, the term *Messiah* is explained as the
Jewish word for the anointed one—that is, the one who has

been acknowledged, as the king or as some other responsible leader, by the religious ritual of pouring over him the sacred, perfumed oil. The literal Greek translation, used here by Mark, is *Christos*, Christ (anointed). Thus the term 'Messiah' or 'Christ' stood for God's chosen and authorized representative in the work of restoring God's People to their true destiny, and in bringing in the kingdom or sovereignty of God; and Peter has dared to admit that he thinks that this is what Jesus is. It was as though one of us had said to a close friend, 'I believe you're really a king in disguise': only, Peter and the others really meant it. They had watched Jesus and were convinced that he was 'different'—a chosen leader, sent and commissioned by God himself.

So far, so good. But Jesus at once tells them to keep this tremendous secret quiet; and begins to talk, not about a victorious king, but about the *Son of Man* (verse 31), who has *to undergo great sufferings. The Son of Man is a term which New* Testament scholars constantly debate about, and it is impossible here to give more than one interpretation—the one which seems to fit the facts best. 'Son of man' is a phrase used in Hebrew poetical passages, and means in itself no more than 'a man', or 'man'. Thus, in Ps. 8: 4, it says:
'What is man that thou shouldst remember him,
mortal man (literally 'the son of man') that thou shouldst care for him?'
Obviously 'man' and 'the son of man' there mean the same.

But in Dan. 7 comes a special use of the phrase. There is an account of a dream in which the dreamer saw, first, four great, nightmare beasts, very frightening and savage. Then he saw an old man (verse 9) sitting, evidently as a judge in some heavenly court; and, as he looked, the last of the fierce beasts was defeated and destroyed; and then there followed a vision (verse 13) of 'one like a (son of) man', who came 'with the clouds of heaven' and was presented before the old man and was honoured and given wide dominion. Later in the chapter (verses 15 ff.) there is an interpretation of the dream. It becomes clear that the beasts symbolize the cruel tyrants who had oppressed the Jews and tried to make them unfaithful to their religion; while that human figure—the one like a Son of Man—represented 'the saints of the Most High', that is, God's loyal few, who had been ready to go to martyrdom rather than deny their faith. And the vision means that that Son of Man, that human figure, those few brave, loyal people, are, in the end, going to be vindicated in the heavenly court, and given dominion in spite of having suffered martyrdom—indeed, precisely *because of* this faithfulness even to the length of death.

That vision in Dan. 7 probably related originally to the terrible period of the Maccabaean martyrs (about 167 B.C.; see note on 2: 16). But it is quite understandable that if Jesus borrowed the phrase the Son of Man—the human figure—as a symbol, appropriate to his own days and his own work, it stood for that utter loyalty to God which wins through, not by force of arms, not by killing and conquering, but by its readiness to go, defenceless, even to the length of death. It stands for the sovereignty of absolute devotion to God.

If so, this helps to explain the end of our paragraph. By naming Jesus *Messiah*, Peter meant to call him the triumphant rebel leader, who would throw off the Roman tyranny and establish God's people as an independent state. Peter has 'got something': he has at least seen that Jesus is the key figure in God's kingdom, or sovereignty. And Jesus does not positively refuse the title Messiah; but he tells them to keep it secret— for it would certainly be misunderstood by the public in the 'rebel' sense—and, instead, he himself adopts that other title, the Son of Man, the defenceless sufferer, who wins dominion by utter obedience, not by force of arms. 'But this will never do!' cries the exasperated disciple: 'you must not dream of giving in so tamely!' Instantly, Jesus recognizes the very same test as had come to him at the beginning of his ministry. In Matt. 4: 8–10, the tempter shows him all the kingdoms of the world, and invites him to possess them in the world's way (by force of arms, by violence). 'Begone Satan!' is Jesus's reply;

'Scripture says, "You shall do homage to the Lord your God and worship him alone"'. So now again, Jesus recognizes 'the Satan', 'the Opposition' (see note on 1:9–13): '*Away with you, Satan,*' he said; '*you think as men think, not as God thinks.*' Several times already we have seen Jesus trying to keep his great authority a secret: now we gain some insight into the reason for this secrecy. He must at all costs fight the idea that victory is by the kind of Messiahship or kingship which the general public want. He must prepare his disciples to recognize their role as 'the saints of the Most High'—the absolutely loyal even to the length of death; and they must accept Jesus as their leader along this road, not along that other.

34–8. Once this note of 'the suffering Son of Man' has been sounded, it is repeated, to a wider audience.

34. *he must take up his cross.* This does not mean what Christian piety has sometimes suggested—a brave shouldering of heavy trials; it means treating one's very life as forfeit. People carrying crosses were people going to execution. To follow Jesus means to budget for the loss of one's very life. It is by no means improbable that Jesus had already foreseen that it would be by the Roman death of crucifixion that he himself would be executed.

35. *Whoever cares for his own safety is lost.* The non-Christian poet-scholar, A. E. Housman, called these words the most important truth ever uttered, the greatest discovery ever made in the moral world; but in saying this he did not go on to consider the words *for my sake and for the Gospel.* Jesus calls not merely for a negative self-abandonment, but for a positive devotion to him and the good news he brings.

38. *the Son of Man...when he comes in the glory.* The same imagery of final vindication as in Dan. 7: 10, 13–14 (see notes at the head of this section).

9: 1. There is much speculation about the meaning of this. In view of the deliberate time-connexion in verse 2, *Six days later*, it is attractive to take it as an allusion to the transfiguration (see next section), coming in a week's time. In that case, the transfiguration is here interpreted as a kind of preview of *the kingdom of God already come in power*. On the other hand, the saying more naturally means simply that the kingdom of God, in all its power, was going to come before the whole of Jesus's own generation had died. This is exactly like 13: 30, 'I tell you this: the present generation will live to see it all.' In that case, either the coming of the kingdom of God is identified with the events that followed the death of Jesus—the rise of the Christian Church; or else it was a miscalculation to expect it within that generation. We have already seen, in the notes on 1: 15, that, in a sense, the kingdom (or reign) of God confronted people in Jesus himself: where he was, there already, in a sense, was the kingdom of God. Thus, we have to reckon with a wide variety of different applications of the idea of the reign of God: (i) God's sovereignty is given effect wherever Jesus is, for he is, in a supreme sense, the bringer of the kingdom; (ii) it is seen wherever any of the disciples gain special insight, as in the transfiguration, into the glory of Jesus's obedience and service to men; (iii) it is brought into a new stage after the death of Jesus in all the events that sprang from this; (iv) it has yet to reach its final and complete expression in the future, and the literal expectation of the kingdom, in *this* sense, within Jesus's own generation was not realized. See introductory note on 13: 1–13. ✳

## THE TRANSFIGURATION

2 Six days later Jesus took Peter, James, and John with him and led them up a high mountain where they were alone;
3 and in their presence he was transfigured; his clothes became dazzling white, with a whiteness no bleacher on
4 earth could equal. They saw Elijah appear, and Moses with him, and there they were, conversing with Jesus.
5 Then Peter spoke: 'Rabbi,' he said, 'how good it is that we are here! Shall we make three shelters, one for you,
6 one for Moses, and one for Elijah?' (For he did not know

what to say; they were so terrified.) Then a cloud ap- 7
peared, casting its shadow over them, and out of the cloud
came a voice: 'This is my Son, my Beloved; listen to
him.' And now suddenly, when they looked around, there 8
was nobody to be seen but Jesus alone with themselves.

On their way down the mountain, he enjoined them 9
not to tell anyone what they had seen until the Son of Man
had risen from the dead. They seized upon those words, 10
and discussed among themselves what this 'rising from
the dead' could mean. And they put a question to him: 11
'Why do our teachers say that Elijah must come first?'
He replied, 'Yes, Elijah does come first to set everything 12
right. Yet how is it that the scriptures say of the Son of
Man that he is to endure great sufferings and to be treated
with contempt? However, I tell you, Elijah has already 13
come and they have worked their will upon him, as the
scriptures say of him.'

＊ 2–8. It is not very profitable to ask just exactly what
happened: did Jesus really become luminous? What kind of
light was it? Did it throw shadows? Where did Moses and
Elijah spring from? These are questions which Peter, James,
and John themselves probably could not have answered even
at the time. They only knew that they had been through an
overwhelming and indescribable experience which gave them
a new insight into the majestic splendour of Jesus's position and
character—it put him, very literally, 'in a new light'. They
saw him associated with two of the very greatest men of
Israel's past history—Moses, the supreme Lawgiver, and
Elijah, that most commanding of Prophets. Then, at the
climax, there came a cloud—by which the Jews often meant
the mysterious presence of God himself—and a voice, and
then, lo and behold! Jesus absolutely alone.

Perhaps it meant that the Law and the Prophets were being summed up and surpassed in Jesus, God's Son: he, by himself, is the completion and crown of what we now call the Old Testament revelation. But there is no written book of the Old Testament attributed to Elijah: he is not the most obvious figure to represent the prophetic writings (Isaiah would have been more natural). These two figures may perhaps represent not so much the Law and the Prophets as the announcers of the End—forerunners of the fulfilment of God's purposes in Jesus and, in some sense, of the coming of the kingdom of God (see note on 9: 1 and see *Elijah must come first*, 9: 11). There is some evidence that such a function for Moses and Elijah was in keeping with Jewish expectation; for Elijah, at any rate, there is the famous passage, Mal. 4: 5: 'Look, I will send you the prophet Elijah before the great and terrible day of the LORD comes.' The fact that both figures were, in the Old Testament, described as having ended their lives on earth in a mysterious way (Deut. 34: 6; 2 Kings 2: 11) adds to the appropriateness of their mysterious reappearance in this preview of the glorious climax of Jesus's ministry.

2. *a high mountain*: possibly Mount Hermon, over 9000 feet above sea-level, and about twelve miles from Caesarea Philippi (see 8: 27).

7. *This is my Son, my Beloved.* As at the baptism of Jesus (see note on 1: 11), so here, there comes a divine declaration that Jesus is, in a special sense, God's Son. *Listen to him*: in Deut. 18: 18 Moses quotes what God has said to him: 'I will raise up for them a prophet like you...I will put my words into his mouth', and then (verse 19) '...if anyone does not listen to the words which he will speak in my name I will require satisfaction from him'. *Listen to him* seems, thus, to mean: 'Jesus is that mighty successor to Moses, to whom you must listen with special attention.'

9–13. At Caesarea Philippi (see 8: 27–33) Jesus had refused to let Peter call him 'Christ' or 'Messiah' (see notes on 1: 15 and at the head of 8: 27 — 9: 1) without ordering the disciples

to keep it quiet, and adding the martyr-title 'the Son of Man'.
And now here again Jesus urges the three to tell nobody about
what they had seen, *until the Son of Man had risen from the dead*:
again 'the Son of Man'; again the expectation of suffering and
death. As for Elijah, if he is expected to be the forerunner—he
*must come first* (see note on verses 2–8)—the most realistic interpretation of that, Jesus tells them, is not the terrific vision they
have just seen, but the hard facts of the martyrdom of John
the Baptist, his forerunner in actual history. So the vision is
'brought down to earth', not by denying its reality but by
showing what it means: devoted toil, suffering, death. It is
noteworthy that the Greek word here translated *transfigured*
and applied to Jesus, is, elsewhere in the New Testament,
applied also to Christians, as they let God transform their lives
in costly obedience to Christ: 'Adapt yourselves no longer
to the pattern of this present world, but let your minds be re-
made and your whole nature thus transformed' (Rom. 12:2);
'...we all reflect as in a mirror the splendour of the Lord; thus
we are transfigured into his likeness...' (2 Cor. 3: 18). ✻

### THE EPILEPTIC BOY; RETURN FROM THE NORTH: PREPARING FOR THE CLIMAX

When they came back to the disciples they saw a large 14
crowd surrounding them and lawyers arguing with them.
As soon as they saw Jesus the whole crowd were overcome 15
with awe, and they ran forward to welcome him. He 16
asked them, 'What is this argument about?' A man in the 17
crowd spoke up: 'Master, I brought my son to you. He is
possessed by a spirit which makes him speechless. When- 18
ever it attacks him, it dashes him to the ground, and he
foams at the mouth, grinds his teeth, and goes rigid. I
asked your disciples to cast it out, but they failed.' Jesus 19
answered: 'What an unbelieving and perverse generation!

How long shall I be with you? How long must I endure
20 you? Bring him to me.' So they brought the boy to him;
and as soon as the spirit saw him it threw the boy into
convulsions, and he fell on the ground and rolled about
21 foaming at the mouth. Jesus asked his father, 'How long
has he been like this?' 'From childhood,' he replied;
22 'often it has tried to make an end of him by throwing him
into the fire or into water. But if it is at all possible for
23 you, take pity upon us and help us.' 'If it is possible!'
said Jesus. 'Everything is possible to one who has faith.'
24 'I have faith,' cried the boy's father; 'help me where faith
25 falls short.' Jesus saw then that the crowd was closing in
upon them, so he rebuked the unclean spirit. 'Deaf and
dumb spirit,' he said, 'I command you, come out of him
26 and never go back!' After crying aloud and racking him
fiercely, it came out; and the boy looked like a corpse; in
27 fact, many said, 'He is dead.' But Jesus took his hand and
raised him to his feet, and he stood up.

28    Then Jesus went indoors, and his disciples asked him
29 privately, 'Why could not we cast it out?' He said,
'There is no means of casting out this sort but prayer.'

30 They now left that district and made a journey through Gali-
31 lee. Jesus wished it to be kept secret; for he was teaching
his disciples, and telling them, 'The Son of Man is now to
be given up into the power of men, and they will kill him,
and three days after being killed, he will rise again.' But they
32 did not understand what he said, and were afraid to ask.

\* 17. *possessed by a spirit.* See note on 1:21-8. The symptoms
of the fits here described seem to be those of what is now called
epilepsy.

19. When Jesus shows impatience or 'anger and sorrow' (3: 5), it is because of the extraordinary slowness of people to believe what God can do.

24. *I have faith...help me where faith falls short.* This lad's cure is closely connected with his father's ability to trust God, just as in 2: 5 the paralysed man is helped by the faith of his friends. The father has a little faith, but he knows he needs far more of it, and is honest enough to say so.

29. *no means...but prayer.* Whatever wavering faith the father had, needed to be met and reinforced by Jesus's own complete and trustful reliance on God—his confident, believing prayer. It was here, apparently, that the disciples had failed.

30–1. Once again (see note on 9: 9–13), Jesus tries to explain his sort of kingship. His royal authority consists not in coercing others but in respecting their freedom: his royal bounty goes to the length of giving up his own life, when people misunderstand and hate him. The disciples are frightened, and themselves fail to understand. The trouble ahead dismays them; *he will rise again* is something that they cannot in the least grasp. See also 10: 32–4. ✳

VARIOUS SAYINGS: 9: 33 — 10: 31

SAYINGS ON DISCIPLESHIP

So they came to Capernaum; and when he was indoors, 33 he asked them, 'What were you arguing about on the way?' They were silent, because on the way they had been 34 discussing who was the greatest. He sat down, called the 35 Twelve, and said to them, 'If anyone wants to be first, he must make himself last of all and servant of all.' Then he 36 took a child, set him in front of them, and put his arm round him. 'Whoever receives one of these children in 37 my name', he said, 'receives me; and whoever receives me, receives not me but the One who sent me.'

38  John said to him, 'Master, we saw a man driving out
devils in your name, and as he was not one of us, we tried
39  to stop him.' Jesus said, 'Do not stop him; no one who
does a work of divine power in my name will be able the
40  next moment to speak evil of me. For he who is not
41  against us is on our side. I tell you this: if anyone gives you
a cup of water to drink because you are followers of the
Messiah, that man assuredly will not go unrewarded.

42  'As for the man who is a cause of stumbling to one of
these little ones who have faith, it would be better for him
to be thrown into the sea with a millstone round his neck.
43  If your hand is your undoing, cut it off; it is better for you
to enter into life maimed than to keep both hands and go
45  to hell and the unquenchable fire. And if your foot is your
undoing, cut it off; it is better to enter into life a cripple
47  than to keep both your feet and be thrown into hell. And
if it is your eye, tear it out; it is better to enter into the
kingdom of God with one eye than to keep both eyes and
48  be thrown into hell, where the devouring worm never
dies and the fire is not quenched.

49  'For everyone will be salted with fire.

50  'Salt is a good thing; but if the salt loses its saltness, what
will you season it with?

'Have salt in yourselves; and be at peace with one
another.'

\* 33–7. On true greatness. This story is a measure of the
disciples' failure to understand. They are still estimating 'greatness' by grandness. Jesus says: real greatness means caring
about people—not people who are regarded as 'important',
but simply people, such as this child here. If you can see that

Jesus, or God himself, comes to you in some small child—
that is greatness. Jesus was one of the first ever to see how
essentially precious any person is, particularly a young child.
A concern for children was not invented by the welfare state:
it goes back to the teaching of Jesus; see also 10: 13–16.

38–41. *The test of loyalty*. It is all too easy to expect everyone to do things your way, and to join your circle. Jesus says
No: the test is what a man is doing and aiming at. It is true
that one must take sides, for or against God and his chosen
representative: 'He who is not with me is against me...'
(Matt. 12: 30); but, apart from that, do not compel anyone to
go your own particular way.

41 *I tell you this*. The saying seems to go better with
verse 37. It is difficult to relate it to what immediately pre-
cedes, or, indeed, to find a plausible setting for it during the
ministry of Jesus himself. Perhaps it grew up in the early
church, after the followers of Jesus had begun to be called
Christ's (Messiah's) men—Christians, as in Acts 11: 26.

42–8. Some stern sayings about our heavy responsibility
towards any who look up to us; and about the need for a
ruthless determination to sacrifice even what is most precious
for the sake of real life.

43. *life* here must mean 'eternal life'—that is, a right
relation with God. See notes on 10: 17–31.

*go to hell*. The word translated *hell* here is literally *Gehenna*,
a Greek form of the Hebrew words for 'Valley of Hinnom'.
This was a valley to the south of Jerusalem, which had once
been used for grim pagan rites of human sacrifice (Jer. 7: 31,
etc.). King Josiah put an end to this (2 Kings 23: 10), and,
according to a medieval writer, it became a kind of city
incinerator where offal and rubbish were constantly burning.
Thus the name later began to be used symbolically for permanent destruction and decay and for all that was the reverse
of life and joy—sometimes for torment and punishment after
this life (e.g. in the Book of Enoch). So, when Jesus speaks
of the inescapable responsibility for choosing, he uses these

absolute alternatives: it is either 'life' (in the fullest sense) or 'Gehenna' (annihilation or continual burning). Verse 48 emphasizes this by the phrase (derived from Isa. 66: 24): *where the devouring worm never dies and the fire is not quenched.* Verses 44, 46, containing the same phrase, are omitted because they are not in all the manuscripts and were probably added by later scribes.

49–50. Apparently, the only reason why these three sayings are placed here side by side is that they all contain the word 'salt'. We no longer know their original setting, and, without this, it is almost impossible to guess their meaning. Especially, *salted with fire* is an unintelligible phrase. But in Matt. 5: 13 the saying about the saltness of salt is applied to the disciples: 'You are salt to the world....' *

A QUESTION ON DIVORCE

**10** On leaving those parts he came into the regions of Judaea and Transjordan; and when a crowd gathered round him once again, he followed his usual practice and taught
2 them. The question was put to him: 'Is it lawful for a man
3 to divorce his wife?' This was to test him. He asked in
4 return, 'What did Moses command you?' They answered,
'Moses permitted a man to divorce his wife by note of
5 dismissal.' Jesus said to them, 'It was because your minds
6 were closed that he made this rule for you; but in the beginning, at the creation, God made them male and
7 female. For this reason a man shall leave his father and
8 mother, and be made one with his wife; and the two shall become one flesh. It follows that they are no longer two
9 individuals: they are one flesh. What God has joined together, man must not separate.'
10     When they were indoors again the disciples questioned

him about this matter; he said to them, 'Whoever di- 11
vorces his wife and marries another commits adultery
against her: so too, if she divorces her husband and marries 12
another, she commits adultery.'

✻ 4. *Moses permitted a man to divorce his wife.* In Deut. 24: 1 ff.
there is a law that, if a woman is divorced and marries another
man and is then divorced again, the original husband must not
re-marry her. In the course of the law, the grounds for
divorce are described thus: '(if) she does not win his favour
because he finds something shameful in her'. This clause
had been interpreted by the Jews with varying degrees of
laxity or strictness; but Jesus, not taking sides on this issue
at all, goes right behind this law to first principles. Moses's
law, he says, was at best only an effort to bring some sort of
order and restraint into an unteachable society. Ideally, there
should be no question of divorce at all; for God's original
design was that a man and his wife should *be made one*: and
what God has thus created into a single being, man ought
never to divide. That is the real ground for the absolute and
lifelong faithfulness of man and wife. In Matt. 5: 32 and 19: 9
there are versions of a saying of Jesus in which it is implied
that unchastity in the wife is a legitimate ground for divorce;
but it is questionable whether Jesus himself ever gave this
detail of legislation: it is more like Jesus simply to declare the
basic principle. The real parallel to this passage in Mark is in
Matt. 19: 6, which is not legislation, but is a quite uncompro-
mising statement of an ideal. The Christian ideal, then, is
absolutely clear: unbroken, lifelong, exclusive faithfulness.
What particular legislation, in an immoral and chaotic society,
will best help us back to this ideal is another matter. Jesus was
not himself a lawgiver.

12. *if she divorces her husband.* This presupposes Roman law:
it was not something that Jewish law contemplated at all. ✻

### SAYINGS ON ENTRY INTO THE KINGDOM

13 They brought children for him to touch. The disciples
14 rebuked them, but when Jesus saw this he was indignant, and said to them, 'Let the children come to me;
do not try to stop them; for the kingdom of God belongs
15 to such as these. I tell you, whoever does not accept the
16 kingdom of God like a child will never enter it.' And he
put his arms round them, laid his hands upon them, and
blessed them.

17   As he was starting out on a journey, a stranger ran up,
and, kneeling before him, asked, 'Good Master, what
18 must I do to win eternal life?' Jesus said to him, 'Why do
you call me good? No one is good except God alone.
19 You know the commandments: "Do not murder; do not
commit adultery; do not steal; do not give false evidence;
20 do not defraud; honour your father and mother."' 'But,
Master,' he replied, 'I have kept all these since I was a boy.'
21 Jesus looked straight at him; his heart warmed to him, and
he said, 'One thing you lack: go, sell everything you have,
and give to the poor, and you will have riches in heaven;
22 and come, follow me.' At these words his face fell and he
went away with a heavy heart; for he was a man of great
wealth.

23   Jesus looked round at his disciples and said to them,
'How hard it will be for the wealthy to enter the kingdom
24 of God!' They were amazed that he should say this, but
Jesus insisted, 'Children, how hard it is to enter the king-
25 dom of God! It is easier for a camel to pass through the
eye of a needle than for a rich man to enter the kingdom
26 of God.' They were more astonished than ever, and said

to one another, 'Then who can be saved?' Jesus looked at 27
them and said, 'For men it is impossible, but not for
God; everything is possible for God.'

At this Peter spoke. 'We here', he said, 'have left 28
everything to become your followers.' Jesus said, 'I tell 29
you this: there is no one who has given up home, brothers
or sisters, mother, father or children, or land, for my sake
and for the Gospel, who will not receive in this age a 30
hundred times as much—houses, brothers and sisters,
mothers and children, and land—and persecutions besides;
and in the age to come eternal life. But many who are first 31
will be last and the last first.'

* 13. *the disciples rebuked them.* Jesus is indignant that anyone
should think children unimportant. See note on 9: 33–7.

15. *whoever does not accept the kingdom of God like a child.*
Precisely what is meant by *like a child* is not clear. Perhaps the
point is that God's reign can only be received by those who
know that they are utterly dependent on God, as small children are on their parents: they cannot earn it or deserve it or
make it, but only accept it thankfully as God's gift. For *the
kingdom of God* see notes on 1: 15 and 9: 1.

16. This passage has, for obvious reasons, often been connected with the baptism of infants. What it shows, however,
is that, whether or not baptism of infants is right, at any rate
Jesus loved and received children and prayed for blessings on
them.

17–27. Jesus warns his followers that possessions can be a
prison. This attractive inquirer, to whom Jesus's heart
warmed, was a thoroughly good and upright person: he had
always lived a good life. What he lacked was a readiness to
take risks, to give up the security of wealth; he was not the
sort of person who is so warm-hearted in his concern for others

that he does not stop to calculate what it will cost him. His very question is about getting: *what must I do to win eternal life?* Jesus put his finger on the trouble: You cannot *have* real life— eternal life (see note on 9: 43)—without being ready to *lose* life (see note on 8: 35); and the stranger failed to pass this test. Jesus points the moral with a fantastic proverb: it is easier to thread a needle with a great big camel than to get into the kingdom of God when you are bursting with riches. However, he adds, God can release the rich man from his attachment to his possessions. It has often happened: people like St Francis of Assisi have suddenly caught sight of the love of God, and possessiveness has been at an end. There is nothing to show, however, that Jesus's only prescription for possessions is, give them all away! Always, he tells us not to be attached to them. But, sometimes, rich men may have to keep their riches and bear the burden of using them wisely for the kingdom of God.

18. *Why do you call me good? No one is good except God alone.* Perhaps Jesus wants to call a halt to the man's thoughtless flattery. Man, as man, cannot be wholly and absolutely good. When Christians, on other and excellent grounds, had come to recognize that Jesus was *God in man*, they began to find it hard to imagine that he had ever questioned his own absolute goodness. So Matthew has a modified form: "'Good?" said Jesus. "Why do you ask me about that?"' (Matt. 19: 17).

28-31. The reward for detachment: if you do give everything up in obedience to God, is there any compensation? Jesus was never afraid of speaking in terms of reward and penalty; but these were never fixed artificially. They always sprang inevitably out of the action in question. Anyone who surrenders the securities of life in obedience to some call to service is promised real life *in the age to come*. That is not compensation for loss in this life: it is a quality of life that can only be entered into by one who dares, as it were, to swim in deep waters. And, incidentally, that quality of life begins to be experienced here and now, even in the circumstances of the transitory world; even here, he finds a wonderfully deep bond of fellowship and friendship among those for whom and with whom he works. An Albert Schweitzer, surrendering all the prospects of what is usually called advancement and success, gains instead the gratitude and friendship of countless patients in Lambarene hospital, not to mention the thousands elsewhere. A few such people actually win recognition from the world at large; but usually the world's judgements will turn out to be topsy turvy: *many who are first will be last and the last first.* ✳

# *Challenge to Jerusalem*

✳ This title, given by the New English Bible to the section 10: 32 — 13: 37, is meant to suggest that Jesus's journey to Jerusalem and his last days there were a final attempt to rouse the religious leaders to accept the reign of God as it was offered them in Jesus. It is a section full of fierce controversy. ✳

### MORE SAYINGS; BLIND BARTIMAEUS

THEY WERE on the road, going up to Jerusalem, Jesus leading the way; and the disciples were filled with awe, while those who followed behind were afraid. He took the Twelve aside and began to tell them what was to happen to him. 'We are now going to Jerusalem,' he said; 'and the Son of Man will be given up to the chief priests and the doctors of the law; they will condemn him to death and hand him over to the foreign power. He will be mocked and spat upon, flogged and killed; and three days afterwards, he will rise again.'

James and John, the sons of Zebedee, approached him and said, 'Master, we should like you to do us a favour.'

36, 37 'What is it you want me to do?' he asked. They answered, 'Grant us the right to sit in state with you, one at your
38 right and the other at your left.' Jesus said to them, 'You do not understand what you are asking. Can you drink the cup that I drink, or be baptized with the baptism I am
39 baptized with?' 'We can', they answered. Jesus said, 'The cup that I drink you shall drink, and the baptism I
40 am baptized with shall be your baptism; but to sit at my right or left is not for me to grant; it is for those to whom it has already been assigned.'

41      When the other ten heard this, they were indignant
42 with James and John. Jesus called them to him and said, 'You know that in the world the recognized rulers lord it over their subjects, and their great men make them feel
43 the weight of authority. That is not the way with you; among you, whoever wants to be great must be your
44 servant, and whoever wants to be first must be the willing
45 slave of all. For even the Son of Man did not come to be served but to serve, and to give up his life as a ransom for many.'

46      They came to Jericho; and as he was leaving the town, with his disciples and a large crowd, Bartimaeus son of Timaeus, a blind beggar, was seated at the roadside.
47 Hearing that it was Jesus of Nazareth, he began to shout,
48 'Son of David, Jesus, have pity on me!' Many of the people told him to hold his tongue; but he shouted all the
49 more, 'Son of David, have pity on me.' Jesus stopped and said, 'Call him'; so they called the blind man and
50 said, 'Take heart; stand up; he is calling you.' At that he
51 threw off his cloak, sprang up, and came to Jesus. Jesus said to him, 'What do you want me to do for you?'

'Master,' the blind man answered, 'I want my sight back.' Jesus said to him, 'Go; your faith has cured you.' 52 And at once he recovered his sight and followed him on the road.

* * *

\* 32–4. This is another warning (see note on 9: 30–2). Jesus again tries to explain to his followers the cost of what he is going to do, and again comes the incredible expectation, *he will rise again.*

35–45. Jesus tells the disciples that he is going to give up his life for others. Just as at Caesarea Philippi (see 8: 27–33) Peter had misunderstood the role of Jesus and had actually rebuked him for thinking of giving up his life, so here again two leading followers of Jesus—James and John—miss his meaning so hopelessly that they come and ask for the most important places in the privy council, so to speak, of the kingdom they imagine Jesus is going to set up. They are still blind to Jesus's idea of royal glory which means, not coercing and tyrannizing and snatching power, but giving and giving with such royal bounty that in the end one's very life is given. Jesus tries to explain by using the grim analogies of *the cup* and *baptism*. The cup is the symbol of a bitter and terrible 'drink' of trouble:

The LORD holds a cup in his hand...
and all the wicked on earth must drain it to the dregs (Ps. 75: 8);

...Jerusalem. You have drunk from the LORD's hand the cup of his wrath (Isa. 51: 17).

And *baptism*, though we so often forget this in Christian baptism, really means a drowning deluge of trouble. Can James and John face their share of these? 'Yes', they say, 'we can'—little knowing what they are saying. Jesus patiently replies that they are right—for he looks forward to a future when they will have entered so fully into his spirit that they will indeed be ready to pay the price; but, even so, it is not for him to bestow high office in the kingdom of God. That is a matter already arranged by God. Just possibly there is meant to be here an ironic hint that, when Jesus 'reigns on the cross' it will be not his disciples who appear on his left and right—they will all have run away. Instead, it will be the two wretched bandits who were crucified with him. At any rate, the other close friends of Jesus, hearing of the impertinent request of James and John, are indignant—showing, by their jealousy, that they, too, are thinking in terms of promotion. So Jesus has patiently to start all over again and explain that these ideas of honour and grandness are topsy turvy: true greatness—the only greatness recognized in the kingdom of God—is the greatness of service: why, the Son of Man himself came, not to be waited on but to wait on others, and to surrender his own life to rescue others. For *the Son of Man*, see note on 8: 27—9: 1.

*45. to give up his life as a ransom for many.* The idea that a martyr's death may purchase release for others is expressed in 4 Maccabees, which is an account of the famous Jewish martyrs of the Maccabaean period (about 200–100 B.C.), written, possibly, later than the time of Jesus, and not included in the ordinary English editions of the Apocrypha. For instance, in 4 Macc. 17: 21 the martyrs are described as having made restitution for the nation's sin. The martyr's death was thus thought to win favour with God and so release the nation from his displeasure. But in this saying of Jesus—which may or may not be an echo of Isa. 53: 10 '...who had made himself a sacrifice for sin' (literally: 'a guilt-offering')—we ought not to press the question, to whom is this ransom paid? It is certainly not a New Testament idea that God, in a mercenary way, demands 'recompense'. The point of the present saying is evidently that Jesus sees the death of *one* individual, himself, as leading to benefit for *many*. It is one of the very few sayings in this Gospel, and the only one thus far, which

84

states the meaning and purpose of the approaching surrender of his life. His is to be a self-giving whose benefits will be of incalculable extent. Christians pondering afterwards on the meaning of the death of Christ recognized it as indeed *all-inclusive*: Paul writes, 'As in Adam all men die, so in Christ all will be brought to life' (1 Cor. 15: 22).

46–52. Compare with this the previous story about a blind man, in 8: 22–6. There is no good reason for not understanding it literally; but it incidentally provides a perfect picture of how a man comes to God. The blind man, yearning for a full life and conscious of his miserable handicap, realizes that here is someone who can help. With complete simplicity and straightforwardness he trusts Jesus, calls him *Son of David*—that is, the descendant of the ideal King of Israel, the royal deliverer who would rescue his people—and makes his request expectantly. He is given sight, and he follows Jesus, full of gratitude.

52. *your faith has cured you*: once again, this emphasis shows that this is a matter of personal relationship, not impersonal magic. See note on 5: 25–34. *

JESUS RIDES INTO JERUSALEM

They were now approaching Jerusalem, and when they **11** reached Bethphage and Bethany, at the Mount of Olives, he sent two of his disciples with these instructions: 'Go to **2** the village opposite, and, just as you enter, you will find tethered there a colt which no one has yet ridden. Untie it and bring it here. If anyone asks, "Why are you doing **3** that?", say, "Our Master needs it, and will send it back here without delay."' So they went off, and found the **4** colt tethered at a door outside in the street. They were untying it when some of the bystanders asked, 'What are **5** you doing, untying that colt?' They answered as Jesus **6** had told them, and were then allowed to take it. So they **7**

brought the colt to Jesus and spread their cloaks on it, and
8 he mounted. And people carpeted the road with their
cloaks, while others spread brushwood which they had
9 cut in the fields; and those who went ahead and the others
who came behind shouted, 'Hosanna! Blessings on him
10 who comes in the name of the Lord! Blessings on the
coming kingdom of our father David! Hosanna in the
heavens!'
11    He entered Jerusalem and went into the temple, where
he looked at the whole scene; but, as it was now late, he
went out to Bethany with the Twelve.

* Thus far, Jesus has tried very hard indeed to prevent people
talking about him as Messiah or King of Israel: see 8: 27–33.
Now, by what seems to have been a carefully prearranged
plan, he takes care that he *shall* be so acclaimed. He has a
young animal fetched (Matt. 21: 2 and John 12: 15 say it was
a donkey colt) and deliberately rides into Jerusalem, letting the
crowds escort him like royalty, in a triumphant procession.
What is the meaning of this extraordinary action? It was
Passover time, and Passover (see note on 14: 1) was the Jewish
festival at which the expectations of God's deliverance always
reached fever-heat among the huge crowds of pilgrims who
came to Jerusalem from all over the world to celebrate the
festival. It might seem as though Jesus was deliberately asking
for trouble: after keeping his position so secret for so long, he
now does something calculated to touch off a nationalist ex-
plosion. And yet, it all ends quietly: *he went out to Bethany with
the Twelve* (verse 11). Can the explanation lie—though this
is only a guess—in the fact that he deliberately led the triumphal
procession *into the temple* (verse 11)? The way to whip up a
nationalist mob might have been either to storm the Roman
garrison or to go to some other quarter, where the Romans
would not quickly be able to suppress them. But the temple

was neither the garrison itself, nor yet out of reach of it; it was actually overlooked by the Roman garrison which, at dangerous times like Passover time, was always well-manned. Was Jesus, perhaps, saying by this, 'Yes: I *am* Messiah; but not *your* sort of Messiah. I am leading a rebellion, but not against the Romans; I am leading an attack on what is wrong at the very heart of your own religion'? See verses 15–19. It is in keeping with this that the accounts, already referred to, in Matt. 21: 1 ff. and John 12: 12 ff. associate the event with an Old Testament passage: 'Rejoice, rejoice, daughter of Zion, shout aloud, daughter of Jerusalem; for see, your king is coming to you, his cause won, his victory gained, humble and mounted on an ass, on a foal, the young of a she-ass' (Zech. 9: 9). This seems originally to have described a triumphant deliverer coming to Jerusalem (Zion) after some great victory, for 'just, and having salvation' might better be rendered 'vindicated and victorious'. He is 'lowly' in the sense that he comes in peace, not with a view to battle; and we are not to picture the donkey as a rather ludicrous mount, as it might be in England, for 'in the East' (writes G. A. Smith, *The Book of the Twelve Prophets*, II (1928), p. 456), 'asses are used...by great officials, but only when these are upon civil, not military duty'. Jesus seemed to his friends, as they recollected the scene, to have ridden into Jerusalem like that: as Messiah, as Deliverer, but as a peaceful one, not in the guise of a warrior. 'I *am* Messiah', he had seemed to say, 'but not the warrior-Messiah whom you are looking for.'

9. *Hosanna!* This represents a Hebrew word meaning *O save!* which comes, among other places, in Ps. 118: 25. But it had come to be not only a prayer to God for help but also a shout of triumph; and it is with this mixture of meanings that the excited crowds greet the man they think is the longed-for king at last, the Messiah chosen by God to save them from Roman oppression. ✳

### THE FIG-TREE AND THE PURGING OF THE TEMPLE

12 On the following day, after they had left Bethany, he felt
13 hungry, and, noticing in the distance a fig-tree in leaf, he
went to see if he could find anything on it. But when he
came there he found nothing but leaves; for it was not the
14 season for figs. He said to the tree, 'May no one ever
again eat fruit from you!' And his disciples were listening.
15    So they came to Jerusalem, and he went into the temple
and began driving out those who bought and sold in the
temple. He upset the tables of the money-changers and
16 the seats of the dealers in pigeons; and he would not allow
anyone to use the temple court as a thoroughfare for
17 carrying goods. Then he began to teach them, and said,
'Does not Scripture say, "My house shall be called a
house of prayer for all the nations"? But you have made
18 it a robbers' cave.' The chief priests and the doctors of the
law heard of this and sought some means of making away
with him; for they were afraid of him, because the whole
19 crowd was spellbound by his teaching. And when evening
came he went out of the city.
20    Early next morning, as they passed by, they saw that the
21 fig-tree had withered from the roots up; and Peter, recalling what had happened, said to him, 'Rabbi, look, the
22 fig-tree which you cursed has withered.' Jesus answered
23 them, 'Have faith in God. I tell you this: if anyone says
to this mountain, "Be lifted from your place and hurled
into the sea", and has no inward doubts, but believes that
24 what he says is happening, it will be done for him. I tell
you, then, whatever you ask for in prayer, believe that
you have received it and it will be yours.

25   'And when you stand praying, if you have a grievance
against anyone, forgive him, so that your Father in heaven
may forgive you the wrongs you have done.'


✲ 14. It is very odd that Jesus should condemn a fig-tree for
having no fruit when it was not even the season for fruit. See
below, note on 11: 20-5. For the moment, note only the
placing of these two sections about the fig-tree (12-14, 20-5)
on either side of another section, namely the purging of the
temple (15-19).

15-19. It has to be remembered that the temple, though
indeed a building for worship, was quite unlike a Christian
Church or a Jewish synagogue (see note on 1: 21). The temple
was for worship through the *action* of animal sacrifice; so it was
elaborately arranged, with large open courts and altars and
drainage systems and so forth, for the very messy and bloody
business of slaughtering animals for sacrifice, burning parts of
them, and cooking and eating other parts. This had, not un-
naturally, led to the growth of a kind of market on the spot,
where worshippers could buy their animals; and, since custom
demanded that temple-dues should be paid, not in the detested
Roman coinage but in the nearest available equivalent to the
old Hebrew shekel, the money-changers also had their stalls
there.

This, though understandable enough, had no doubt turned
the outer court of the temple into a noisy, haggling market-
place. As well as being unseemly for the vestibule to the altar,
this took up a great deal of room in the only court where
non-Jews were allowed to come to pay their respect to the
God of the Jews, and where they ought to have been made
welcome. It was meant to be *a house of prayer for all the nations*
(verse 17—the quotation is from Isa. 56: 7). It may be for
both these reasons that Jesus took drastic action. He accused
them of turning God's house of prayer into a robbers' hide-out
(the allusion is to Jer. 7: 11), and he swept them all out. Rough?

Dangerous? Yes: but perhaps the only gesture they could understand. It is the natural sequel to the triumphal entry if this is interpreted (see note on 11: 1–11) as an acted parable, meaning: 'the true Messiah's mission is to purge the temple of avarice, not the country of Romans'.

18. The religious authorities are furious and plan to kill him. John's Gospel tells the story of the purging of the temple at the beginning of Jesus's ministry, and attributes the climax of antagonism at the end rather to Jesus's raising of Lazarus from death (see John 2: 13 ff.; 11: 45 ff.).

20–5. Scene two of the story of the fig-tree. For scene one, see verses 12–14. Only Mark thus divides the story of the fig-tree by the story of the purging of the temple; Matthew and Luke arrange things differently. It has been suggested that Mark's arrangement is to underline the lesson that the fig-tree's failure and doom means the failure of the Jewish nation to rise to its opportunities, and the doom that is going to follow—the purging of the temple providing a vivid picture of the rottenness of Jewish religion. Certainly the *parable* of the barren fig-tree in Luke 13: 6–9 seems to carry this message. It seems that we must look on the story of the withered fig-tree here either as the story of something that actually happened and that provided a parable of the nation's state, or as a story designed to describe, in picture-language, the state of the nation. But on any showing it is very odd that Jesus should be described as blasting a tree, and that the narrator should go out of his way to 'excuse' the tree on the ground that figs were not in season (verse 13). It is easy to find destructive wonders in the late fictions about the life of Jesus known as the apocryphal Gospels. But in the accounts of Jesus in the New Testament there is practically no parallel. As for 'excusing' the tree, this spoils the allegory (for the Jewish nation *ought* to have 'borne fruit') and also makes the story even more problematic. It has been ingeniously suggested that what actually happened was that Jesus, meditating on Israel's failure, uttered the old Prophet's symbolic phrase (Mic. 7: 1) 'there are no grapes left to eat, none of those early figs that I love', and then, as a grim, prophetic, acted parable, did actually cause the tree to wither; while the disciples, overhearing the words from Micah, thought that Jesus was literally hungry, and, in telling the story afterwards, recorded their surprise, remarking that figs were not really in season. Or again, it has been suggested that possibly Jesus genuinely hoped for figs; being disappointed, he turned his frustration into a prophetic saying against Jerusalem; and subsequently (as it happened!) the tree withered. All these suggestions seem more or less far-fetched; but it is hard to find a more satisfactory explanation.

Still more difficult is the use of this destructive miracle as an example of splendid faith, to reinforce the lesson that there is nothing too difficult for prayer to achieve. Perhaps we may guess that the evangelist, or the tradition on which he drew, has here put together bits and pieces of scattered incidents and sayings into a shape which does not correspond either with the mind of Jesus or with the actual facts.

26. *But if you do not forgive others, then the wrongs you have done will not be forgiven by your Father in heaven.* Omitted here because it is not in all the manuscripts and was probably added by later scribes who recalled the words from Matt. 6: 15. ✲

JESUS'S AUTHORITY CHALLENGED;
THE ALLEGORY OF THE VINEYARD

They came once more to Jerusalem. And as he was 27 walking in the temple court the chief priests, lawyers, and elders came to him and said, 'By what authority are you 28 acting like this? Who gave you authority to act in this way?' Jesus said to them, 'I have a question to ask you 29 too; and if you give me an answer, I will tell you by what authority I act. The baptism of John: was it from God, or 30 from men? Answer me.' This set them arguing among 31 themselves: 'What shall we say? If we say, "from God",

32 he will say, "Then why did you not believe him?" Shall we
say, "from men"?'—but they were afraid of the people,
33 for all held that John was in fact a prophet. So they answered, 'We do not know.' And Jesus said to them,
'Then neither will I tell you by what authority I act.'

**12**    He went on to speak to them in parables: 'A man
planted a vineyard and put a wall round it, hewed out a
winepress, and built a watch-tower; then he let it out to
2 vine-growers and went abroad. When the season came,
he sent a servant to the tenants to collect from them his
3 share of the produce. But they took him, thrashed him,
4 and sent him away empty-handed. Again, he sent them
another servant, whom they beat about the head and
5 treated outrageously. So he sent another, and that one they
killed; and many more besides, of whom they beat some,
6 and killed others. He had now only one left to send, his
own dear son. In the end he sent him. "They will respect
7 my son", he said. But the tenants said to one another,
"This is the heir; come on, let us kill him, and the pro-
8 perty will be ours." So they seized him and killed him,
9 and flung his body out of the vineyard. What will the
owner of the vineyard do? He will come and put the
tenants to death and give the vineyard to others.

10    'Can it be that you have never read this text: "The
stone which the builders rejected has become the main
11 corner-stone. This is the Lord's doing, and it is wonderful
in our eyes"?'

12    Then they began to look for a way to arrest him, for
they saw that the parable was aimed at them; but they
were afraid of the people, so they left him alone and
went away.

☆ After his high-handed purging of the temple, it is not surprising that Jesus was challenged by the religious authorities to produce his credentials. As he had often done before (see 2: 9, 19, 25ff.; 3: 4, 23; 10: 3), he asked a counter-question—not in order to evade an answer, but because the most effective answer is the one which one's opponent is forced to acknowledge by his own thinking. So he asked them what kind of authority they attached to John the Baptist's work (see notes on 1: 1–8). The authorities knew perfectly well that John the Baptist was a genuine prophet, sent by God—or, even if they thought otherwise, they knew that this was the conviction of most people; and they knew that Jesus, in the same way but even more so, undeniably carried the marks of his genuine authority in his life and person. To save face, therefore, they had to say '*We do not know*', and were met by the inevitable rejoinder from Jesus.

12. 1–12. Seizing the initiative he had just gained, Jesus tells a story with a very thinly veiled allegorical meaning. The vineyard is Israel, as in the Old Testament allegory in Isa. 5: 1–7 ('I will sing for my beloved my love-song about his vineyard...'). In Isaiah, the well-cultivated vineyard produced nothing but miserable, sour wild grapes; in Jesus's story things are even worse—the tenants turn criminal and beat up each successive messenger from the owner till, at the climax, they actually kill his own son. Anyone can guess the sort of reprisals that must follow. It is clear enough that Jesus meant that the Jews, who were supposed to be God's representatives and to do his work in the world, had turned selfish and had refused to listen to his messengers the prophets. The climax of the story suggests that Jesus foresaw also that they were even going to reject and kill God's own Son; and that the disasters which were going to follow would be what they had brought upon themselves by this atrocious deed. More than once, the Gospels show Jesus as keenly sensitive to the political situation and well aware that the nation was heading for the disastrous clash with Rome which in fact led

to the destruction of the temple some years later, in A.D. 70. Some of the parables of Jesus may have been adapted by later preachers to the conditions of their own time. This story, so clearly directed against the irresponsible religious leaders of his own day, seems to furnish an example of a genuinely contemporary, unaltered piece of Jesus's teaching. Some scholars even question whether the reference to the son was meant by Jesus to be an allusion to himself, and treat it as just the climax of the story. In that case, we have a simple *parable* rather than an allegory (see note on 4: 1-34 for the distinction), making the single point that the nation has rejected God's messengers and will have to face the consequences. It seems more likely, however, that Jesus was consciously alluding to his unique function. In that case, it is a brief allegory, and the veiled self-reference by Jesus is as striking as it is rare in this Gospel.

10. *this text*: it is in Ps. 118: 22—the very same Psalm from which the jubilant *hosanna*-cry came (see note on 11: 9). The meaning of the proverb is clear enough, and it is used by Christians afterwards with reference to Jesus's vindication (see Acts 4: 11; 1 Pet. 2: 7). ✻

## QUESTION AND ANSWER

13 A number of Pharisees and men of Herod's party were
14 sent to trap him with a question. They came and said, 'Master, you are an honest man, we know, and truckle to no one, whoever he may be; you teach in all honesty the way of life that God requires. Are we or are we not
15 permitted to pay taxes to the Roman Emperor? Shall we pay or not?' He saw how crafty their question was, and said, 'Why are you trying to catch me out? Fetch me a
16 silver piece, and let me look at it.' They brought one, and he said to them, 'Whose head is this, and whose inscrip-
17 tion?' 'Caesar's', they replied. Then Jesus said, 'Pay

Caesar what is due to Caesar, and pay God what is due to
God.' And they heard him with astonishment.

Next Sadducees came to him. (It is they who say that 18
there is no resurrection.) Their question was this: 'Master, 19
Moses laid it down for us that if there are brothers, and
one dies leaving a wife but no child, then the next should
marry the widow and carry on his brother's family. Now 20
there were seven brothers. The first took a wife and died
without issue. Then the second married her, and he too 21
died without issue. So did the third. Eventually the seven 22
of them died, all without issue. Finally the woman died.
At the resurrection, when they come back to life, whose 23
wife will she be, since all seven had married her?' Jesus 24
said to them, 'You are mistaken, and surely this is the
reason: you do not know either the scriptures or the power
of God. When they rise from the dead, men and women 25
do not marry; they are like angels in heaven.

'But about the resurrection of the dead, have you 26
never read in the Book of Moses, in the story of the
burning bush, how God spoke to him and said, "I am the
God of Abraham, the God of Isaac, and the God of
Jacob"? God is not God of the dead but of the living. 27
You are greatly mistaken.'

Then one of the lawyers, who had been listening to 28
these discussions and had noted how well he answered,
came forward and asked him, 'Which commandment is
first of all?' Jesus answered, 'The first is, "Hear, O Israel: 29
the Lord our God is the only Lord; love the Lord your 30
God with all your heart, with all your soul, with all your
mind, and with all your strength." The second is this: 31
"Love your neighbour as yourself." There is no other

32 commandment greater than these.' The lawyer said to
him, 'Well said, Master. You are right in saying that God
33 is one and beside him there is no other.  And to love him
with all your heart, all your understanding, and all your
strength, and to love your neighbour as yourself—that is
34 far more than any burnt offerings or sacrifices.' When
Jesus saw how sensibly he answered, he said to him, 'You
are not far from the kingdom of God.'

After that nobody ventured to put any more questions
35 to him; and Jesus went on to say, as he taught in the temple,
'How can the teachers of the law maintain that the Mes-
36 siah is "Son of David"?  David himself said, when inspired by the Holy Spirit, "The Lord said to my Lord,
'Sit at my right hand until I put your enemies under your
37 feet.'"' David himself calls him "Lord"; how can he also
be David's son?'

\* 13-17.  The next round in this bitter contest is started by
a joint attack by *Pharisees and men of Herod's party*, who try to
trap Jesus with a question about whether to pay taxes to the
Roman government.  For the Pharisees, see note on 2: 16; and
for the Herodians, see notes on 3: 6 and 8: 15.  It was an
unnatural alliance, for the aims of these two groups were
normally very different.  But, in their different ways, both
were nationalists, opposed to Rome.  If, in reply to their
question, Jesus advocated paying taxes, they could thus make
him exceedingly unpopular with their partisans.  On the other
hand, they hated Jesus so much that, if he advocated a revolt
against the Roman system they would have no hesitation in
denouncing him to the Roman governor as a rebel.  Either
way, they would win.  Jesus made no pretence of not seeing
through them: *Why are you trying to catch me out?* he asks.  And
then, characteristically, he proceeds to get them to answer

their own question. *Fetch me a silver piece.* This was the Roman coin in which the tax was paid; and the very fact that they were able to produce one suggested that they were not particularly serious in debating whether to pay it or not. When the coin is brought, Jesus only has to ask whose head and inscription it bears to lead them to admit that it is Caesar's coinage; and to accept and use the currency is to put oneself under an obligation to the government which administers it: *Pay Caesar what is due to Caesar* is the logical consequence to their own admission. But, having won, Jesus then seizes the opportunity to add the penetrating phrase: *and pay God what is due to God.* It has been suggested that what is implied is that man, who bears God's image (Gen. 1: 27, 'God created man in his own image'), is owed to God as much as the coin bearing Caesar's image is owed to Caesar. Obedient dedication to God is not necessarily incompatible with obedient citizenship—though there are times when the two clash.

18-27. Jesus is asked a second trap question about resurrection. The Sadducees were another Jewish group. Their name sounds like the Hebrew for 'the righteous ones' and it could also be associated with the Zadokites, an ancient High-priestly family (see 2 Sam. 8: 17, etc.). The Sadducees were the High-priestly aristocracy of Judaism. Unlike the Pharisees (for whom see note on 2: 16) they did not rely on oral tradition or entertain modern theological beliefs. They kept to the scriptures, and had no belief in an after-life. Perhaps it would not be true to say that, originally, their ancestors had aims which were very different from those of the ancestors of the Pharisees; but, as the aristocracy, it was the Sadducees who had to negotiate with the aliens, and they had trimmed their sails to the prevailing wind, learnt how to compromise, and grown wealthy out of it. If it was different with the Pharisees, this may have been partly because their less exalted social position made it easier for them to get away without compromise. The Sadducees came of parents who had stayed in office by judicious bribery and political astuteness; and their hatred of Jesus now

97

was due to their fear of an innovator who might be a rebel and might uncomfortably rock the boat.

The question they asked was a well-known joke—a way of trying to make the Pharisaic belief in resurrection and life after death look absurd.

19. *Moses laid it down*: in Deut. 25: 5–10, and compare Ruth 4: 5. This is called the Levirate Law (from Latin *levir*, brother-in-law). How widely it was actually in force at various periods and in various areas is not certain.

25. Jesus's reply is in two parts. First, he says that life after death is bigger than the limited relations of this life, and therefore is not at all disproved by assuming the ludicrous situation that would arise if it meant a mere perpetuation of the same conditions that prevail on earth. The exclusive loyalty of husband and wife in this life may prove to be a way forward into a wider and more inclusive fellowship in that other life.

26–7. Then, secondly, he appeals to the permanent character of fellowship with the living God as a guarantee of survival. The Old Testament phrase *I am the God of Abraham*, etc. (Exod. 3:6) need, of course, mean no more than 'I am the God whom Abraham *used* to worship'; but Jesus takes it as a description of a relationship into which God had called Abraham: and death cannot break a relationship thus begun. The Sadducees are reckoning without their God: that is the long and short of it.

28–34*a*. Whether this teacher of the law or scribe (see note on 1: 22), who was so impressed by Jesus, asked this question about the first commandment with a genuine desire to learn, or simply to test Jesus, is not clear. We only know that the scribes did debate about the relative 'weight' of various commandments in the Books of Moses and that it was a question demanding courage and depth to answer well. Jesus's reply is absolute and unhesitating: 'Love God' is the greatest of all the commandments, and 'Love your neighbour'—that is, your fellow-man—is the next; and nothing whatever must be allowed to come before them. This meant that all the elaborate and twisty casuistry like the 'corban law' alluded to in 7: 9–13 is simply swept aside. Jesus puts personal devotion —to God and to man—right in front; and the student of the law frankly agrees: the whole Jewish sacrificial system is nothing compared with this. Jesus declares that what the man has said shows him to be very near to the kingdom of God (see note on 1: 15).

29. *Hear, O Israel.* This phrase, calling attention to a solemn announcement, comes in Deut. 6: 4, from which this commandment to love God is quoted. The Hebrew for 'Hear!', *Shema*, thus came to be the title for this recitation of duty, and we speak of the Jewish *shema*, rather as we give the name 'creed' to a confession of faith beginning (in Latin) with *credo*, 'I believe'. The other law—love of neighbour—is from Lev. 19: 18.

34b–37. Left victorious in this battle of wits, with no other opponent daring to challenge him, Jesus, in his turn, puts a hard question. The Messiah—the anointed one (see notes on 1: 15 and 8: 27 — 9: 1)—the divinely appointed king for whom the nation longed, was expected to come from the family of King David. Now, Psalm 110 was agreed to be by David. Whether it actually is, is not here relevant. Authorship by David was what Jesus and his contemporaries all, rightly or wrongly, assumed. And it was also assumed to contain an address to the Messiah. Now, says Jesus, in that Psalm David, alluding to this future royal figure, uses the words 'The LORD said to my lord...'. In other words, David calls the Messiah 'my lord': how, then, can that Messiah be David's junior— his son? The answer intended by Jesus would seem to be 'Because, although he is his son by descent and therefore his junior in age, he is also, in some mysterious way, superior to David and therefore his senior in rank'. It was a way of saying that the Messiah is more than an ordinary human descendant of a Jewish royal house, and that therefore the Jews should not be so prosaic and blind and conservative as not to be ready to learn from the extraordinary things that were confronting them wherever Jesus went: see note on 1: 21 — 2: 12. ✳

### CONDEMNATION OF THE RELIGIOUS TEACHERS; THE WIDOW'S FARTHING

38 There was a great crowd and they listened eagerly. He said as he taught them, 'Beware of the doctors of the law, who love to walk up and down in long robes, receiving
39 respectful greetings in the street; and to have the chief
40 seats in synagogues, and places of honour at feasts. These are the men who eat up the property of widows, while they say long prayers for appearance' sake, and they will receive the severest sentence.'

41 Once he was standing opposite the temple treasury, watching as people dropped their money into the chest.
42 Many rich people were giving large sums. Presently there came a poor widow who dropped in two tiny coins,
43 together worth a farthing. He called his disciples to him. 'I tell you this,' he said: 'this poor widow has given more
44 than any of the others; for those others who have given had more than enough, but she, with less than enough, has given all that she had to live on.'

☀ 38. For *doctors of the law* see note on 1: 22.

There is no evidence that all the theologians of Jesus's time were frauds, using their position merely as a cloak for cruelty and greed. Indeed, in 12: 28–34a we have just met an apparently sincere and honest one. But the most influential of them seem to have conceived a bitter hatred of Jesus, and one can only guess that this was because they were indeed using their powers selfishly and irresponsibly and detested his exposure of their real motives. Matt. 23 contains a longer version of this fierce attack on them.

The religious teachers have just been accused of growing

rich by cruelly robbing the defenceless widows; perhaps that is why Mark has added here this exquisite little story of a widow who gave away the minute copper coins which were the whole of her savings, to the temple fund—a way of expressing gratitude to God. Jesus recognized there the finest gift of the day. *

### LOOKING INTO THE FUTURE: 13: 1–37

* This famous chapter is often called 'the little apocalypse'. 'Apocalypse', which is the Greek for 'unveiling' or 'revelation', is a technical term for writings which claim to be a peep behind the scenes, as it were—a view of the secret purposes of God. This type of literature has a long history in Judaism before Jesus. Within the Old Testament itself, the book of Daniel contains some apocalyptic material, and there were plenty of Jewish 'apocalypses' outside the Old Testament. In the New Testament, the longest continuous piece of apocalyptic writing is the book called the Revelation of John; but there are parts of other New Testament books belonging to the same class: 2 Thess. 2 is a famous example, and Mark 13 is another. The parallels in Matt. 24 and Luke 21 should be studied side by side with our chapter, but it is not possible here to go into the details of the differences or the various suggestions about the origin of these sections. Very briefly, it may be said that some scholars think that all or most of this chapter came from some Christian prophet's tract, written after the death of Jesus but delivered in his name and sincerely believed to be inspired by Jesus himself. Others think that it is a patchwork of genuine sayings of Jesus, but that it was not Jesus who put them together in this pattern; while others again are ready to believe that, substantially, it is as he spoke it.

Apart from problems of detail, there are two particular difficulties about it:

(i) Can we really believe that Jesus himself thought in this bizarre and fantastic way about the future? Did he really expect signs and portents in the sky and the sudden winding-up of history by some single, instantaneous, supernatural event (see verses 24–7)?

(ii) Although, in verse 32, it says that only God knows the *precise* moment when this is going to happen, verses 30–1 say emphatically that, at any rate, it will all happen within that very generation. But that was more than 1900 years ago, and still nothing like it seems to have taken place. Are we to think that Jesus made a vast mistake?

In reply to problem (i) it may be said that—whether or not Jesus himself spoke this chapter just as it stands—this kind of picture-language must not be taken literally. It must be understood as a way of saying, 'There is much more to human history than the things done by men: there are factors bigger than human, and, in the end, all is in the hand of God, who has his plans and will have the last word when he has brought history to the end of its course.' And you cannot speak effectively about what is bigger than human without calling in language different from the normal—language about the sun failing, stars falling, and so forth. And although it is perfectly clear that Jesus took human history very seriously, lived in the present, and believed that God's reign was very intimately concerned with men's choices and decisions there and then, it would be surprising, all the same, if he never used startling language pointing to these other, more than human aspects of it. In a sense, such 'future' and 'above-human' language is the only way in which to explain the tremendous importance of the present and the human.

Regarding (ii), although the evangelist makes it very clear that where Jesus was, there, in a unique sense, was God, it is equally clear that Jesus was a real man; and his actual *knowledge* was limited, however unlimited may have been his penetrating wisdom and understanding of people and his perfect harmony with God. It may be, then, that he was actually mistaken in expecting the end of things so soon. If he was, it still would not alter all that is implied by the evidence for his unique nearness to God and the unique nearness of God's reign in him.

Or again, in a manner of speaking, he might have been absolutely right if he said what verses 30–1 say; for there is a sense in which great prophets see so clearly and expect so eagerly that they get the perspective, as it were, foreshortened. God's purposes are so plain to them, and what might happen, if only men responded, so real, that they see it all as already all but here: and that may be the only way in which they can tell the truth. Or, yet again, it might be that the dramatic events at the coming of the Holy Spirit are here intended: Acts 2:17 ff. uses very similar language to describe what had by then actually taken place; and that was, of course, easily within that generation. But we still have to reckon with the possibility that they are the words of some later writer, wrongly attributed to Jesus. However, it is to be noted that 9: 1 is in some respects similar: see the note there.  ✻

PRELIMINARIES

As he was leaving the temple, one of his disciples ex- **13** claimed, 'Look, Master, what huge stones! What fine buildings!' Jesus said to him, 'You see these great 2 buildings? Not one stone will be left upon another; all will be thrown down.'

When he was sitting on the Mount of Olives facing the 3 temple he was questioned privately by Peter, James, John, and Andrew. 'Tell us,' they said, 'when will this happen? 4 What will be the sign when the fulfilment of all this is at hand?'

Jesus began: 'Take care that no one misleads you. Many 5, 6 will come claiming my name, and saying, "I am he"; and many will be misled by them.

'When you hear the noise of battle near at hand and the 7 news of battles far away, do not be alarmed. Such things are bound to happen; but the end is still to come. For 8

nation will make war upon nation, kingdom upon kingdom; there will be earthquakes in many places; there will
be famines. With these things the birth-pangs of the new
age begin.

9    'As for you, be on your guard. You will be handed over
to the courts. You will be flogged in synagogues. You
will be summoned to appear before governors and kings
10 on my account to testify in their presence. But before the
11 end the Gospel must be proclaimed to all nations. So
when you are arrested and taken away, do not worry
beforehand about what you will say, but when the time
comes say whatever is given you to say; for it is not you
12 who will be speaking, but the Holy Spirit. Brother will
betray brother to death, and the father his child; children
will turn against their parents and send them to their
13 death. All will hate you for your allegiance to me; but the
man who holds out to the end will be saved.

✻ 1–2. The whole discourse starts from the warning that the
glorious temple was doomed. Such a prediction did not need
divine foreknowledge: a shrewd political observer could have
seen the way things were going.

5–13. Before saying anything further about the temple
itself, Jesus describes the kind of events that are to precede the
disaster:

(i) Verses 5–6, there will be false claimants to messiahship—
for that is what *I am he* seems to mean. We have no evidence
of actual false Messiahs between the death of Jesus and the fall
of Jerusalem in A.D. 70; but a false claim to be a unique
representative of God's presence is near to a false claim to
messiahship; and that is exemplified by the charlatan Simon
the sorcerer in Acts 8: 9.

(ii) Verses 7–8, the whole world will be unsettled by wars
and by disasters such as earthquakes and famines.

(iii) Verses 9–13, Christians will be persecuted, and must rely on the help of the Holy Spirit and persevere in loyalty. ✻

### POLITICAL CLIMAX; ANOTHER WARNING; THE FINAL EVENT

'But when you see "the abomination of desolation" 14 usurping a place which is not his (let the reader understand), then those who are in Judaea must take to the hills. If a man is on the roof, he must not come down into the 15 house to fetch anything out; if in the field, he must not 16 turn back for his coat. Alas for women with child in 17 those days, and for those who have children at the breast! Pray that it may not come in winter. For those days will 18, 19 bring distress such as never has been until now since the beginning of the world which God created—and will never be again. If the Lord had not cut short that time of troubles, 20 no living thing could survive. However, for the sake of his own, whom he has chosen, he has cut short the time.

'Then, if anyone says to you, "Look, here is the 21 Messiah", or, "Look, there he is", do not believe it. Impostors will come claiming to be messiahs or prophets, 22 and they will produce signs and wonders to mislead God's chosen, if such a thing were possible. But you be on your 23 guard; I have forewarned you of it all.

'But in those days, after that distress, the sun will be 24 darkened, the moon will not give her light; the stars will 25 come falling from the sky, the celestial powers will be shaken. Then they will see the Son of Man coming in the 26 clouds with great power and glory, and he will send out the 27 angels and gather his chosen from the four winds, from the farthest bounds of earth to the farthest bounds of heaven.

\* Verses 14–20 forecast the political climax.

14. *'the abomination of desolation'* is in quotation marks because it is a phrase from Dan. 11:31; 12:11 ('the abominable thing that causes desolation', cf. also Dan. 9:27). There, it probably refers to a heathen altar—and, quite likely, an idol also—set up in the temple in 168 B.C. by the tyrant Antiochus Epiphanes. This is described in 1 Macc. 1:54 as 'the abomination of desolation'. Indeed, the Hebrew words may be a deliberate pun on the title of a heathen god—'Zeus of the heavens'. Thus the phrase came to be a recognized way of hinting at any heathen desecration. In A.D. 40, the Roman Emperor Caligula attempted to have his statue placed in the temple. Those who find the origin of Mark 13 in a Christian prophet's utterance might trace the use of the phrase to this, and date it accordingly. But it could be a general reference to the desecration of the temple by the Romans whenever Jerusalem fell, as ultimately happened in A.D. 70.

*usurping a place which is not his.* Strikingly, what began as an impersonal phrase (*abomination* being a neuter noun in Greek) runs on into personal terms (*usurping* is a masculine participle in the Greek). It is perhaps meant to suggest that, behind whatever 'abomination' is meant, there is the Roman Emperor or some personal opponent of God on the demonic level and on the more than human scale.

(*let the reader understand*). This is evidently a note, put in when this passage was written down, to call the reader's attention to the cypher-language and remind him to interpret it.

*those who are in Judaea must take to the hills.* This seems, again, to be a general term, meaning little more than just 'escape': hills often have caves in them, and, anyway, it is easier to escape from troops among hills than on the plain. In recent years, caves in the Judaean hills near the Dead Sea have been discovered in which Jewish refugees hid at the time of the later Jewish revolt of A.D. 132–5. The flight to the hills was also made by the followers of Mattathias and his family, who came to be known as the Maccabees; cf. 1 Macc. 2:28. When the

Christian colony in Jerusalem did escape at the time of the
siege, it appears that they went all the way to Pella, which is in
Transjordan and is not in particularly hilly country.

20. *for the sake of his own, whom he has chosen, he has cut short
the time.* All through the Bible runs the idea that God has
chosen out a People—Israel—from the rest of men, and that he
champions and protects and rescues them. But this is not the
favouritism it might seem to be. In the first place, to God's
'choice' corresponds man's response, so that God's 'chosen'
People are, in fact, not just the lucky ones, but those who have
taken the trouble to answer the call which God makes to *all*
men. And, secondly, the call itself is not a call to safety and
security but to the service of others; and it is precisely the
failure to recognize the duties involved in it that leads to that
doom and rejection of Jerusalem which is here being foretold.

*his own, whom he has chosen,* who are rescued and for whose
sake the distress is limited, are evidently those who respond
to the challenge of Jesus.

21-3. Another warning; see note on 13: 5-13. If the
arrangement of these sayings is deliberate, we must take this as
a warning that, *after* the political climax (the fall of Jerusalem),
there will be *further* false claimants to messiahship. In A.D. 132
there was, as it happens, a conspicuous one, who called himself
Simeon ben Koseba, and was known to his admirers as bar
Kokhba (Son of a Star).

24-7. The final event. As has already been said (see note on
apocalyptic writing at the head of this chapter, on pp. 101 ff.),
there really is no other way, except this kind of picture-
language, to allude to events which are bigger than human—
all that lies, as a believer in God knows, behind and above
history as well as within it.

26. *the Son of Man coming in the clouds.* See notes on
8: 27 — 9: 1. *In the clouds* is a clear reference to the vision in
Dan. 7: 13, and is evidently a symbol for exaltation, or more
than human status. This is the final vindication of that 'human
figure' which, in Daniel, symbolizes the Jews who are faithful

even to the length of martyrdom, and which Jesus accepted as the symbol for his own function and purpose.

27. *his chosen.* See note on 13: 20. ✳

### EXHORTATION TO BE READY

28 'Learn a lesson from the fig-tree. When its tender shoots appear and are breaking into leaf, you know that summer
29 is near. In the same way, when you see all this happening,
30 you may know that the end is near, at the very door. I tell you this: the present generation will live to see it all.
31 Heaven and earth will pass away; my words will never pass away.

32 'But about that day or that hour no one knows, not even the angels in heaven, not even the Son; only the Father.

33 'Be alert, be wakeful. You do not know when the
34 moment comes. It is like a man away from home: he has left his house and put his servants in charge, each with his own work to do, and he has ordered the door-keeper to
35 stay awake. Keep awake, then, for you do not know when the master of the house is coming. Evening or midnight,
36 cock-crow or early dawn—if he comes suddenly, he must
37 not find you asleep. And what I say to you, I say to everyone: Keep awake.'

✳ This chapter ends with a challenge to the disciples to be ready, delivered in three main points:

(i) The disciples would be able to recognize the signs that these events were on the way as easily as they might recognize the signs of spring's approach; and it was going to happen within that generation.

(ii) But the precise moment is a secret to everyone but God himself.

(iii) Therefore, they must show great alertness and readiness, like faithful servants, left by their master to be ready for his sudden return.

**31.** *my words will never pass away.* In judging of this statement, see the note on apocalyptic writing, particularly (ii), pp. 102-3.

**32.** *not even the Son; only the Father.* The unqualified use of the words, *the Son, the Father,* is common from the time when Christians had reached clear convictions about the unique relation of Jesus, the perfect Son of God, to the heavenly Father. Does this mean that Jesus did not himself use such language? It is impossible to say that he could not himself have used it (compare the ending of the parable of the vineyard in 12: 1-12, and the notes there, p. 94); and, if it were a later addition, from the period of full conviction about Jesus's divinity, is it likely that it would have been attached to this statement that there was something that even the Son of God did not know? On the question of the limits of his knowledge, see, again, the note on apocalyptic writing, particularly (ii), pp 102-3. ✶

# *The Final Conflict*

## PLOTTING AND DEVOTION

NOW THE FESTIVAL of Passover and Unleavened **14** Bread was only two days off; and the chief priests and the doctors of the law were trying to devise some cunning plan to seize him and put him to death. 'It must **2** not be during the festival,' they said, 'or we should have rioting among the people.'

3 · Jesus was at Bethany, in the house of Simon the leper. As he sat at table, a woman came in carrying a small bottle of very costly perfume, pure oil of nard. She broke it 4 open and poured the oil over his head. Some of those present said to one another angrily, 'Why this waste? 5 The perfume might have been sold for thirty pounds and the money given to the poor'; and they turned upon her 6 with fury. But Jesus said, 'Let her alone. Why must you make trouble for her? It is a fine thing she has done for 7 me. You have the poor among you always, and you can help them whenever you like; but you will not always 8 have me. She has done what lay in her power; she is 9 beforehand with anointing my body for burial. I tell you this: wherever in all the world the Gospel is proclaimed, what she has done will be told as her memorial.'

10 · Then Judas Iscariot, one of the Twelve, went to the 11 chief priests to betray him to them. When they heard what he had come for, they were greatly pleased, and promised him money; and he began to look for a good opportunity to betray him.

\* 1-2. The plot against Jesus's life.

1. *the festival of Passover and Unleavened Bread. Passover* is the English translation of a Hebrew term, *pesach*, which sometimes appears as *Pasch* (hence the adjective 'paschal' used in Christian prayers and hymns). It was the ancient Hebrew name for a spring-time festival, connected in Exod. 12 with the wonderful rescue of the Israelites from slavery in Egypt, by God's own action. The festival always brought with it the remembrance of this triumph of God on behalf of his people, and the hope and expectation of similar vindication in the future.

Originally, *the festival . . . of Unleavened Bread* was apparently a separate observance, but the two seem virtually to have become a single festival, lasting for a week. The main feature of the Passover part of the festival was the ritual killing of lambs in the temple, and the feasting on them by households; the main feature of the Unleavened Bread part was the discontinuance of last year's leaven. Leaven is the substance used to make bread rise (see note on 8: 15), and, as it was usually got from a piece left over from yesterday's dough, it provided continuity from one baking to another. When the Jews deliberately went without it for a week, this was a symbol of a break with all the past, including its sin, and a fresh start. This would gain special point if Passover-and-Unleavened Bread was, at that time, the New Year Festival as it evidently was when Exod. 12: 2 was written: 'This month is for you the first of months.' But the Jewish year has not always begun at Passover time, and may not have done so at the time of Jesus.

Huge crowds of pilgrims flocked to Jerusalem to keep the festival. The enemies of Jesus, both the priestly aristocracy (mostly Sadducees—see note on 12: 18–27), and the scribes, or doctors of the law (mostly Pharisees—see notes on 1: 22; 2: 16), were agreed that, if possible, Jesus must be secretly arrested and put away without rousing the crowds.

3–9. A woman pours expensive scent over Jesus. Her action was expressive of tender love and adoration. One of the most remarkable things about the traditions that have gone into the Gospels is their portrait of Jesus in his relations with women. Here is a young unmarried man who moves freely among women—some of them notoriously immoral—who evidently adored him. Yet, he maintains towards them a completely natural, un-prudish purity, respecting them without in the least condoning their way of life or yielding to their temptations. The woman is blamed, on the ground of utilitarian considerations, for wasting such precious stuff. Jesus defends her on the ground that this is a unique occasion and also— introducing a sombre note—that she has hereby performed in advance, ready for his funeral, the usual Jewish act of putting costly ointments on a dead body. He adds that this will be told of wherever the Gospel is preached—a strange phrase for Jesus himself to use and possibly an addition from the Church's later use of the story.

We do not know much about the host or the woman. Besides the virtually exact parallel to this passage in Matt. 26: 6–13, there are two similar passages which, however, differ in details: Luke 7: 36–8 and John 12: 1–8. In Luke 7: 40 the host's name is Simon, but he is not called 'the leper' but a Pharisee; the incident is not located at all; the woman is expressly called a sinner; she pours her precious gift (less elaborately described) over the feet, not the head, of Jesus, mingling her tears with it; and the comments by the host and by Jesus make quite a different point. In John 12, the incident is located at Bethany; the meal is apparently in the home of Martha and Mary and Lazarus (the sisters appear in Luke 10: 38–42; all three appear in the story of the raising of Lazarus from death in John 11); it is this Mary who pours the precious scent over the feet of Jesus; and it is Judas, the traitor, who voices the objection. The chief differences may be tabulated:

| Mark | Matthew | Luke | John |
|---|---|---|---|
| Bethany | Bethany | — | Bethany |
| Simon | Simon | Simon | Martha |
| the leper | the leper | a Pharisee | Mary |
|  |  |  | Lazarus |
| a woman | a woman | a sinful woman | Mary |
| head | head | feet | feet |
| anointing for burial | anointing for burial | a sign of gratitude for forgiveness | anointing for burial |

It must remain a matter of uncertainty whether we are faced with variations of a single story, or with two—or perhaps three—different incidents with certain features in common.

10–11. The betrayal. It is striking (see too 12: 41–4 above) that the story of the woman's uncalculating, lavish act of adoring love is inserted between the allusion (verses 1–2) to the scheming hatred of Jesus's enemies, and the sordid, calculating treachery of Judas (for whom see note on 3: 16). *

## THE LAST SUPPER

Now on the first day of Unleavened Bread, when the 12 Passover lambs were being slaughtered, his disciples said to him, 'Where would you like us to go and prepare for your Passover supper?' So he sent out two of his disciples 13 with these instructions: 'Go into the city, and a man will meet you carrying a jar of water. Follow him, and when 14 he enters a house give this message to the householder: "The Master says, 'Where is the room reserved for me to eat the Passover with my disciples?'" He will show 15 you a large room upstairs, set out in readiness. Make the preparations for us there.' Then the disciples went off, and 16 when they came into the city they found everything just as he had told them. So they prepared for Passover.

In the evening he came to the house with the Twelve. 17 As they sat at supper Jesus said, 'I tell you this: one of you 18 will betray me—one who is eating with me.' At this they 19 were dismayed; and one by one they said to him, 'Not I, surely?' 'It is one of the Twelve', he said, 'who is dipping 20 into the same bowl with me. The Son of Man is going the 21 way appointed for him in the scriptures; but alas for that man by whom the Son of Man is betrayed! It would be better for that man if he had never been born.'

During supper he took bread, and having said the 22 blessing he broke it and gave it to them, with the words:

23 'Take this; this is my body.' Then he took a cup, and
having offered thanks to God he gave it to them; and they
24 all drank from it. And he said, 'This is my blood, the
25 blood of the covenant, shed for many. I tell you this:
never again shall I drink from the fruit of the vine until
that day when I drink it new in the kingdom of God.'

26    After singing the Passover Hymn, they went out to the
27 Mount of Olives. And Jesus said, 'You will all fall from
your faith; for it stands written: "I will strike the shepherd
28 down and the sheep will be scattered." Nevertheless,
after I am raised again I will go on before you into
29 Galilee.' Peter answered, 'Everyone else may fall away,
30 but I will not.' Jesus said, 'I tell you this: today, this very
night, before the cock crows twice, you yourself will
31 disown me three times.' But he insisted and repeated:
'Even if I must die with you, I will never disown you.'
And they all said the same.

\* Verses 12–16 describe the disciples' preparations for the
Passover. Non-residents had to find somewhere, either in
Jerusalem or within a prescribed distance from it, in which to
keep the festival by joining together in the ritual meal with the
Passover lamb as the main dish. Jesus seems to have made
secret plans in advance so that he and his friends might meet,
with the minimum of publicity, in an upstairs room in the city.

17–31. The Last Supper. When the meal comes to be
described, there is, surprisingly, no mention of a lamb at all.
It has been suggested that, after all, it was only an anticipatory
meal, on the day before the Passover (John clearly intends it
to be such: see John 13: 1; 18: 28; 19: 14, 31); or that Jesus
and his friends were observing a different calendar from that
of the orthodox temple authorities, but, possibly, were treated
by the orthodox as too heretical to be allowed a Passover lamb.

What is clear, from Matthew, Mark, and Luke, is that at the

meal in the room upstairs Jesus attached to the bread and the wine, shared out among his friends, a special meaning. The bread he startlingly called his own body; the wine, he said, was his own blood, shed on behalf of many, like that of a sacrificial animal, used in the Jewish ritual of establishing a covenant. And then he made a solemn religious vow, like the Nazirite vow described in Num. 6: 2ff.: he renounced wine or anything made from grapes until the day when he would drink it fresh, and in a new way, after the reign of God had begun. Extraordinary words! He evidently meant that (i) he knew he was on the verge of his death; (ii) his friends must pledge themselves to share with him in all that it meant; (iii) he was absolutely certain that, through it, God's reign would be established.

In other words, to this solemn religious meal, which, whether actually a Passover or not, was certainly in the context of the Passover season, Jesus attached a completely new sense. Passover, as we have seen, was a recalling of the 'exodus'—the going out of the Israelites from slavery in Egypt into the covenant made by Moses in which they were bound in loyalty to God. Jesus declares that the new covenant, to which the Prophet Jeremiah had looked forward (Jer. 31: 31), is now being established, and that the sacrificial victim for its establishment is his own self. A new era is about to begin, it is his death which introduces it, and he is eager to bind his friends into the new community.

From that day to this, wherever the friends of Jesus have met to break bread and pour wine, recalling the words of Jesus and renewing their loyalty by participation, there the kingdom of God has been reaffirmed as coming in the triumphant death of Jesus. 1 Cor. 10, 11 show something of what Paul saw in the practice:

'When we bless "the cup of blessing", is it not a means of sharing in the blood of Christ? When we break the bread, is it not a means of sharing in the body of Christ? Because there is one loaf, we, many as we are, are one body; for it is one loaf of which we all partake (1 Cor. 10: 16, 17).'

'For every time you eat this bread and drink the cup, you proclaim the death of the Lord, until he comes.'

'It follows that anyone who eats the bread or drinks the cup of the Lord unworthily will be guilty of desecrating the body and blood of the Lord (1 Cor. 11: 26, 27).'

26. *the Passover Hymn* after the ending of the meal consisted of Pss. 114 (or 115) to 118.

The regulations for the Passover required pilgrims to spend the night in Jerusalem; but, sooner or later, a 'greater Jerusalem' was defined for this purpose, spreading a certain distance beyond the actual walls.

*the Mount of Olives* was east of Jerusalem, beyond the Kedron ravine, only about half a mile from the wall of the city. It was easily near enough to Jerusalem to count as 'Jerusalem' for purposes of keeping the Passover.

27. *it stands written.* The vision, courage, and hope which light up this scene are all the more striking in view of the conviction that nothing can stop the impending disaster. The reference is to Zech. 13: 7, just as, in verse 18, *one who is eating with me* is an echo of Ps. 41: 9. *

### THE STRUGGLE WITH TEMPTATION

32 When they reached a place called Gethsemane, he said to
33 his disciples, 'Sit here while I pray.' And he took Peter and James and John with him. Horror and dismay came over
34 him, and he said to them, 'My heart is ready to break with
35 grief; stop here, and stay awake.' Then he went forward a little, threw himself on the ground, and prayed that, if
36 it were possible, this hour might pass him by. 'Abba, Father,' he said, 'all things are possible to thee; take this cup away from me. Yet not what I will, but what thou wilt.'
37 He came back and found them asleep; and he said to

Peter, 'Asleep, Simon? Were you not able to stay awake for one hour? Stay awake, all of you; and pray that you 38 may be spared the test. The spirit is willing, but the flesh is weak.' Once more he went away and prayed. On his return 39, 40 he found them asleep again, for their eyes were heavy; and they did not know how to answer him.

The third time he came and said to them, 'Still sleeping? 41 Still taking your ease? Enough! The hour has come. The Son of Man is betrayed to sinful men. Up, let us go 42 forward! My betrayer is upon us.'

* This section portrays Jesus as anything but above temptation. So far from sailing serenely through his trials like some superior being unconcerned with this world, he is almost dead with distress. He prays earnestly to God for escape from the indescribably heavy trial that is coming—from this *cup* of trouble (see note on 10: 35-45). But he is resolved at all costs to accept and do God's will, not his own.

32. *a place called Gethsemane.* According to John 18: 1-2, the place to which Jesus and his disciples went was a garden beyond the Kedron ravine; and Gethsemane (which seems to mean 'olive-press') is generally located on the lower slopes of the Mount of Olives (see note on 14: 26).

36. *Abba* is, in Aramaic, which was the language probably used normally by Jesus, a very intimate form of the word 'Father'. Jewish children used it in addressing their own fathers. Jesus combines trust and intimate love for God, his Father, with perfect, costly obedience. The word was echoed afterwards by Christians: see Rom. 8: 15; Gal. 4: 6.

Jesus's disciples, by contrast, cannot even *stay awake*—far less enter fully into the struggle with him.

41. *Still sleeping? Still taking your ease?* Perhaps the correct translation is, rather, 'Are you going to continue to sleep and take your ease?'

*Enough!* The N.E.B. has a note rightly calling this obscure. The Greek word can mean 'he (*or* it) duly has [something] back(*or* has [something] in full)'. This can be used impersonally to mean 'Enough of this!' ('it [the situation] has nothing more to wait for'); but the same verb in the first person, 'I have duly', is a common form on receipts (= 'received in full'). Hence the (rather far-fetched) suggestion represented by the alternative version in the note, that the verb refers to the traitor Judas, who has received his bribe in full and is on his way: 'The money has been paid in full', 'The account is settled'.

*The hour has come.* In a context like this, as in verse 35, *the hour* means the long foreseen and fateful moment—the moment when loyalty and endurance are going to be strained to breaking-point.

*The Son of Man.* See notes on 8: 27 — 9: 1.

*is betrayed to sinful men. Sinful* here is probably used in the same sense as the word translated 'heathen' in Acts 2: 23, 'you used heathen men to crucify and kill him'. With overwhelming irony, the one who is at the very heart of the truest Jewish loyalty is betrayed to Gentiles!

42. *let us go forward!* If this is the correct interpretation, it will mean that Jesus sees the situation as a great campaign— the battle of the kingdom of God. His friends are summoned to 'advance' like soldiers entering battle. But it is a battle in which Jesus will not use physical force but only the weapon of loyalty to God's will. ✻

THE ARREST

43 Suddenly, while he was still speaking, Judas, one of the Twelve, appeared, and with him was a crowd armed with swords and cudgels, sent by the chief priests, lawyers, and
44 elders. Now the traitor had agreed with them upon a signal: 'The one I kiss is your man; seize him and get him

safely away.' When he reached the spot, he stepped for- 45
ward at once and said to Jesus, 'Rabbi', and kissed him.
Then they seized him and held him fast. 46

One of the party drew his sword, and struck at the 47
High Priest's servant, cutting off his ear. Then Jesus spoke: 48
'Do you take me for a bandit, that you have come out with
swords and cudgels to arrest me? Day after day I was 49
within your reach as I taught in the temple, and you did
not lay hands on me. But let the scriptures be fulfilled.'
Then the disciples all deserted him and ran away. 50

Among those following was a young man with nothing 51
on but a linen cloth. They tried to seize him; but he slipped 52
out of the linen cloth and ran away naked.

* 43. Jesus is arrested by a crudely armed force raised by an
unnatural alliance of Sadducees and Pharisees (see notes on
2: 16 and 12: 18-27). By using Judas (see note on 3: 16) as
guide, they catch Jesus quietly, away from the Passover
crowds (see 14: 1-2).

45. *Rabbi*, literally 'My great one', was a common form
of address to a revered teacher.

*and kissed him.* In Palestine, kissing was a quite normal form
of respectful greeting from one man to another, as it still is
in many countries today. In 2 Sam. 20: 9 another dastardly
deed of treachery is associated, like this one, with a kiss, when
the military leader Joab stabs his rival Amasa while greeting
him.

47. *One of the party.* John 18: 10 says it was Peter.

48. *Do you take me for a bandit...?* The word bandit implies a
guerilla leader, a free-lance leader of a resistance-movement.

49. *let the scriptures be fulfilled*: no doubt the scriptures
intended are such as Ps. 41: 9 and Zech. 13: 7, already alluded
to in 14: 18, 27. Such Old Testament passages served as typical

examples of the way in which, in each succeeding crisis, when the noble were betrayed and the cowardly fled, God achieved his plan for his people through the loyal minority. Jesus knows that the same pattern is now going to be repeated, but in a higher and more intense degree than ever before: now is to be the climax and fulfilment of what the Old Testament had shown in typical examples which were, however, incomplete, and imperfect.

51. *a young man.* We do not know who this was, nor why the strange incident (which has no parallel in Matthew or Luke) is recorded. It is an attractive guess that it was Mark, the evangelist, himself: but that is only a guess. ✳

### JESUS ON TRIAL

53 Then they led Jesus away to the High Priest's house, where the chief priests, elders, and doctors of the law were
54 all assembling. Peter followed him at a distance right into the High Priest's courtyard; and there he remained, sitting among the attendants, warming himself at the fire.

55 The chief priests and the whole Council tried to find some evidence against Jesus to warrant a death-sentence,
56 but failed to find any. Many gave false evidence against
57 him, but their statements did not tally. Some stood up and
58 gave false evidence against him to this effect: 'We heard him say, "I will pull down this temple, made with human hands, and in three days I will build another, not made with
59 hands." 'But even on this point their evidence did not agree.
60 Then the High Priest stood up in his place and questioned Jesus: 'Have you no answer to the charges that
61 these witnesses bring against you?' But he kept silence; he made no reply.

Again the High Priest questioned him: 'Are you the

Messiah, the Son of the Blessed One?' Jesus said, 'I am; 62
and you will see the Son of Man seated at the right hand
of God and coming with the clouds of heaven.' Then the 63
High Priest tore his robes and said, 'Need we call further
witnesses? You have heard the blasphemy. What is your 64
opinion?' Their judgement was unanimous: that he was
guilty and should be put to death.

Some began to spit on him, blindfolded him, and struck 65
him with their fists, crying out, 'Prophesy!' And the
High Priest's men set upon him with blows.

Meanwhile Peter was still below in the courtyard. 66
One of the High Priest's serving-maids came by and saw 67
him there warming himself. She looked into his face and
said, 'You were there too, with this man from Nazareth,
this Jesus.' But he denied it: 'I know nothing,' he said; 68
'I do not understand what you mean.' Then he went outside into the porch; and the maid saw him there again and 69
began to say to the bystanders, 'He is one of them'; and 70
again he denied it.

Again, a little later, the bystanders said to Peter, 'Surely
you are one of them. You must be; you are a Galilean.'
At this he broke out into curses, and with an oath he said, 71
'I do not know this man you speak of.' Then the cock 72
crew a second time; and Peter remembered how Jesus had
said to him, 'Before the cock crows twice you will disown
me three times.' And he burst into tears.


As soon as morning came, the chief priests, having made **15**
their plan with the elders and lawyers in full council,
put Jesus in chains; then they led him away and handed
him over to Pilate. Pilate asked him, 'Are you the king of 2

3 the Jews?' He replied, 'The words are yours.' And the
4 chief priests brought many charges against him. Pilate
questioned him again: 'Have you nothing to say in your
defence? You see how many charges they are bringing
5 against you.' But, to Pilate's astonishment, Jesus made no
further reply.

6    At the festival season the Governor used to release one
7 prisoner at the people's request. As it happened, the man
known as Barabbas was then in custody with the rebels
8 who had committed murder in the rising. When the
9 crowd appeared asking for the usual favour, Pilate replied,
'Do you wish me to release for you the king of the Jews?'
10 For he knew it was out of malice that they had brought
11 Jesus before him. But the chief priests incited the crowd
12 to ask him to release Barabbas rather than Jesus. Pilate
spoke to them again: 'Then what shall I do with the man
13 you call king of the Jews?' They shouted back, 'Crucify
14 him!' 'Why, what harm has he done?' Pilate asked;
15 but they shouted all the louder, 'Crucify him!' So Pilate,
in his desire to satisfy the mob, released Barabbas to them;
and he had Jesus flogged and handed him over to be
crucified.

16    Then the soldiers took him inside the courtyard (the
Governor's headquarters) and called together the whole
17 company. They dressed him in purple, and plaiting a
18 crown of thorns, placed it on his head. Then they began
19 to salute him with, 'Hail, King of the Jews!' They beat
him about the head with a cane and spat upon him, and
20 then knelt and paid mock homage to him. When they had
finished their mockery, they stripped him of the purple
and dressed him in his own clothes.

✻ 53. The trial before the Jewish authorities. There is much discussion about the trial-stories, which vary a good deal from one Gospel to another. Mark gives the impression that there was one, apparently actually during the night, before the Jewish authorities, and a second, the next morning, before the Roman governor.

54. The stage is set for Peter's denial. See below, note on 14: 66–72.

55–65. Attempts to find incriminating evidence fail, and even when the High Priest invites the prisoner to reply, he is dauntingly silent. Only when asked, point-blank, '*Are you the Messiah, the Son of the Blessed One?*' (verse 61) does Jesus at last break his majestic silence. For *Messiah*, see notes on 1: 15 and 8: 27 — 9: 1. *The Blessed One* means God.

62. In 8: 27–33, when Jesus was called 'Christ' (or 'Messiah'), he immediately said something about *the Son of Man* (see notes there). So now, although, according to this version of the story, he does accept the title 'Messiah', he immediately adds a *Son of Man* saying: they are going to see him, Jesus says, like that human figure in Dan. 7, vindicated by God himself, triumphant, and exalted. This tremendous saying is deemed blasphemy—a man making superhuman claims. The presiding High Priest tears his robes as a symbol that something dreadful and irrevocable has happened. Jesus is sentenced to death. There follows an outbreak of coarse jesting and maltreatment by the men who hold him in custody.

66–72. Peter thrice denies all connexion with Jesus. This heart-piercing scene was anticipated in 14: 27–31, and is led up to by steady degrees: first, the sleepy inattention of Peter and the others at the place called Gethsemane (14: 37); then the useless slashing about (14: 47); then the half-hearted following (14: 54).

15: 1–20. The trial before Pilate. The Jewish court have just agreed on the death-sentence for blasphemy, but now, instead of executing the sentence they hand Jesus on to the Roman governor, Pilate. Pilate's question, *Are you the king of the*

*Jews?* (verse 2) suggests that they accused Jesus before him of attempting a nationalist uprising to throw off the Roman yoke and liberate the Jews. Such 'messianic' risings were not uncommon: an instance seems to be that of Barabbas, in verse 7. It is not clear why the Jews altered both the court and the charge. The simplest explanation of why they did not execute Jesus themselves is that, at that period, the Roman government reserved this right for themselves. This has often been disputed; but John 18: 31 certainly implies it, and it makes sense. Another possibility is that the Jewish authorities, knowing the popularity of Jesus with the general Jewish public, deftly shifted the blame for his actual execution on to others. At any rate, if Rome is to be the judge they must find a charge which Rome will consider a crime—the political charge.

The irony of the situation is overpowering: Jesus, who is, indeed, king of the Jews in a deeply spiritual sense, has refused to lead a political uprising. Yet now, condemned for blasphemy by the Jews because of his spiritual claims, he is accused by them also before Pilate for being precisely what he had disappointed the crowds by failing to be—a political insurgent. Jesus refused either to plead guilty or to defend himself.

1. *Pilate*: Pontius Pilate was the Roman governor or prefect of Judaea, A.D. 26–36. We hear about him also from the non-Christian Jewish writers Philo and Josephus, who were about contemporary with the New Testament writers. They both give him a bad character, though one cannot help seeing that he was placed in a very difficult and unenviable position by the turn which events had taken.

6. *At the festival season the Governor used to release one prisoner at the people's request.* It seems highly improbable that the people could really demand a release and choose their man, and there is no external evidence of this custom. Perhaps an amnesty was actually granted in the particular case of Barabbas, and Christian tradition had drawn a false deduction. In any case, the irony is still further increased, when, in place of Jesus, who had refused to lead a rising, an actual insurgent, Barabbas, is released.

Barabbas means 'the son of Abbas'; if his own personal name was Jesus, as appears from Matt. 27: 17, it is the more striking: it is Jesus bar Joseph, the spiritual king of the Jews, over against Jesus bar Abbas, a bandit leader.

13. *Crucify.* To crucify is to put on a cross (Latin *crux*, genitive *crucis*). It was a barbaric practice used by the Romans, among others, in dealing with criminals who were slaves or in some other sense regarded as without rights, to fasten them by ropes or even nails to an upright post, with a cross-bar for the arms, and let them die slowly of exposure and thirst. The Jewish method of execution would have been by stoning (cf. Acts 7: 58: how came it that the Jews on that occasion did execute the death-sentence?).

16–20. Now Jesus is coarsely maltreated by the Roman soldiers, as previously by the Jewish soldiers (see 14: 65).  ✳

THE EXECUTION

Then they took him out to crucify him. A man called 21 Simon, from Cyrene, the father of Alexander and Rufus, was passing by on his way in from the country, and they pressed him into service to carry his cross.

They brought him to the place called Golgotha, which 22 means 'Place of a skull'. He was offered drugged wine, 23 but he would not take it. Then they fastened him to the 24 cross. They divided his clothes among them, casting lots to decide what each should have.

The hour of the crucifixion was nine in the morning, 25 and the inscription giving the charge against him read, 26 'The king of the Jews.' Two bandits were crucified with 27 him, one on his right and the other on his left.

The passers-by hurled abuse at him: 'Aha!' they cried, 29 wagging their heads, 'you would pull the temple down, would you, and build it in three days? Come down from 30

31 the cross and save yourself!' So too the chief priests and
lawyers jested with one another: 'He saved others,' they
32 said, 'but he cannot save himself. Let the Messiah, the
king of Israel, come down now from the cross. If we see
that, we shall believe.' Even those who were crucified
with him taunted him.

33    At midday a darkness fell over the whole land, which
34 lasted till three in the afternoon; and at three Jesus cried
aloud, '*Eli, Eli, lema sabachthani?*', which means, 'My God,
35 my God, why hast thou forsaken me?' Some of the
bystanders, on hearing this, said, 'Hark, he is calling
36 Elijah.' A man ran and soaked a sponge in sour wine and
held it to his lips on the end of a cane. 'Let us see', he
37 said, 'if Elijah will come to take him down.' Then Jesus
38 gave a loud cry and died. And the curtain of the temple
39 was torn in two from top to bottom. And when the
centurion who was standing opposite him saw how he
died, he said, 'Truly this man was a son of God.'

✻  21. *Simon.* The description suggests that his sons were known
to the users of this Gospel.  Had they become Christians?

*pressed him into service.* That is, exercised the right to enlist a
passer-by for forced labour (cf. Matt. 5: 41).  It is not clear
precisely within what limits a Roman soldier could exercise
this right.

22. *Golgotha.* The name means skull in Aramaic.  Calvary,
the better-known name, is from the Latin translation (*calvaria*,
a skull).  Eusebius, the Christian writer mentioned above
(p. 4), placed Golgotha to the north of Mount Zion (the
Temple site); but it is impossible now to be certain of the site.

The offer of *drugged wine* (verse 23) is said to have been a
small act of mercy.  Perhaps the reason why Jesus refused it was
his Nazirite vow at the Last Supper (see note on 14: 17–31).

27. *Two bandits.* Two more like Barabbas.

29. *you would pull the temple down?* According to 14: 58–9, this strange charge was also brought, though unsuccessfully, at the trial. Perhaps predictions of the doom of Jerusalem, as in 13: 2, lie behind it; but John 2: 19 gives more definite shape to it.

33. *darkness.* This is an unexplained portent.

34. *Eli...* This (in one dialect or another) is the opening of Ps. 22. It is difficult to believe that Jesus only quoted these words because they led on to the triumph and confidence with which that Psalm ends. It is more realistic to gain from them an appalling glimpse into the sense of utter defeat and despair which Jesus suffered in obediently accepting that terrible 'cup' of trouble alluded to in 14: 36.

35. Ignorant and heartless bystanders mistook *Eli*, 'my God', for a cry to Elijah, the great Prophet, and turned it into a taunt.

37–9. The tremendous end comes suddenly: *a loud cry*—how surprising from a weakened, dying man!—and a death which, for some reason, quite overwhelmed the pagan soldier who was on duty, in charge of the execution squad. Many crucified people lingered on for days. Jesus appears to have somehow voluntarily given up his life when the right moment came.

38. *the curtain of the temple.* In each of the successive temples in Jerusalem—the one in question was Herod's temple—there had been one or more elaborate curtains, screening the innermost and most holy shrine of all (so 2 Chron. 3: 14, for Solomon's temple) or the room immediately outside this (so a description of Herod's temple in the Jewish historian Josephus's *Jewish War*, v, 212–14). If either of these huge, sacred curtains had been literally ripped in two, whether by human hands or more mysteriously, so dismaying a portent would surely have been mentioned by some historian (e.g. Josephus). But, although Josephus does, indeed, mention strange portents at another time (*Jewish War*, vI, 288 ff.), there is nothing about the veil. When, therefore, Mark says that it was torn, it is, perhaps, his own dramatic, theological comment. At the death

of Jesus, he means, access to the innermost shrine—to the very presence of God—was complete. Thenceforth, without a mediator, without any system of priesthood, anyone who trusts God can come straight into his presence. For he is the God who, as Christians were later to discover, had himself suffered in his own Son for the sake of the very men who caused the suffering. In the same sense, Heb. 10: 19 says: 'the blood of Jesus makes us free to enter boldly into the sanctuary by the new, living way which he has opened for us through the curtain, the way of his flesh' [or '...through the curtain of his flesh'].

39. *a son of God.* 'Jesus, the Son of God' is the theme of the beginning and end of this Gospel (see note on 1: 9-13). It is a very telling and dramatic touch that this confession at the end is on the lips of a pagan soldier. Doubtless, such a man would believe in many gods, and his phrase would not mean more than that this man was, in some sense, divine. The evangelist and the Christian reader see in it a much deeper meaning, and the alternative rendering, 'the Son of God' (N.E.B. footnote, cf. Matt. 27: 54) is grammatically possible. ✶

### THE BURIAL

40 A number of women were also present, watching from a distance. Among them were Mary of Magdala, Mary the mother of James the younger and of Joseph, and Salome,
41 who had all followed him and waited on him when he was in Galilee, and there were several others who had come up to Jerusalem with him.

42 By this time evening had come; and as it was Preparation-day (that is, the day before the Sabbath),
43 Joseph of Arimathaea, a respected member of the Council, a man who looked forward to the kingdom of God, bravely went in to Pilate and asked for the body of Jesus.

Pilate was surprised to hear that he was already dead; so 44
he sent for the centurion and asked him whether it was
long since he died. And when he heard the centurion's 45
report, he gave Joseph leave to take the dead body. So 46
Joseph bought a linen sheet, took him down from the
cross, and wrapped him in the sheet. Then he laid him in
a tomb cut out of the rock, and rolled a stone against the
entrance. And Mary of Magdala and Mary the mother of 47
Joseph were watching and saw where he was laid..

* 40–1. *Mary of Magdala*. All that is known of this woman is
derived from this verse, with verse 47 and 16: 1 (with the
corresponding verses in Matthew, 27: 56, 61; 28: 1), 16: 9–11
(probably based on Luke and John), brief references in Luke
and John, and one extended reference in John. In Luke
8: 1–2, she is among a number of women 'who had been
set free from evil spirits and infirmities' and who 'provided
for' Jesus 'out of their own resources' (cf. Mark 15: 41);
and from Mary, in particular, 'seven devils had come out'
(cf. Mark 16: 9); in Luke 24: 10 she is among the women who
found the tomb empty and told the apostles. In John 19: 25
she is described, with other women, as near the cross (in
contrast to the *watching from a distance* here). The extended
reference is in John 20: 1–18 (cf. Mark 16: 9–11), the exquisite
story of her meeting with the risen Christ. 'Magdalene', the
adjective by which she is described in most English versions
and which appears in so many dedications of Churches and
Colleges, means the same as *of Magdala*, Magdala being, apparently, a town on the west of Lake Gennesaret (cf. Mark
8: 10, note in N.E.B. margin). That this Mary had been cured
of some disorder which might today be called neurotic is clear
from Luke 8: 1–2. But there is no justification for the widely
held notion that she must be identified with the unnamed
disreputable woman of Luke 7: 36–50.

*Mary the mother of James.* This way of distinguishing another Mary suggests that her sons were still known to the Christians among whom these traditions were treasured. Cf. the note on Alexander and Rufus, 15: 21 above.

*Salome.* The parallel verse in Matthew (27: 56) has 'the mother of the sons of Zebedee' as the third woman. If the two traditions are identical, then Salome was the mother (or, conceivably, the step-mother) of James and John (see 1: 19).

42 ff. Little care was normally taken over the corpses of the crucified. But suddenly, a wealthy sympathizer, Joseph of Arimathaea, a member of the Council which had tried Jesus, bravely comes forward, asks to have the body, and gives it a rich man's burial in a rock-tomb with a wheel of stone to close it. Mention has already been made of the surprising speed with which Jesus gave up his life (see note on 15: 37–9); Pilate, too, is surprised.  ✲

### HE IS NOT HERE

**16** When the Sabbath was over, Mary of Magdala, Mary the mother of James, and Salome bought aromatic oils in-
2 tending to go and anoint him; and very early on the Sunday morning, just after sunrise, they came to the
3 tomb. They were wondering among themselves who would roll away the stone for them from the entrance to
4 the tomb, when they looked up and saw that the stone,
5 huge as it was, had been rolled back already. They went into the tomb, where they saw a youth sitting on the right-hand side, wearing a white robe; and they were
6 dumbfounded. But he said to them, 'Fear nothing; you are looking for Jesus of Nazareth, who was crucified. He has been raised again; he is not here; look, there is the
7 place where they laid him. But go and give this message to his disciples and Peter: "He is going on before you into

Galilee; there you will see him, as he told you.'" Then 8
they went out and ran away from the tomb, beside
themselves with terror. They said nothing to anybody, for
they were afraid.

* 16: 1. Jesus was buried on what we call a Friday—the day
before the Jewish Sabbath (see note on 1: 21), which is Satur-
day. As soon as that day of stillness was over, at the earliest
possible moment, the women are at the tomb, determined to
honour the dead as best they may (see note on 14: 3–9):
nowadays it would be by bringing flowers. (The practical-
minded men seem to have stayed away. Perhaps they said
'What's the good?') Very simply the dramatic story is told.
The women were wondering how ever they would remove
that heavy wheel of stone, when, lo and behold!, they saw
that it had already gone. For the rest, there is nothing to equal
Mark's own words.

1. See note on 15: 40–1.
5. *a youth...wearing a white robe.* Evidently Mark means
an angel; but an angel is not the sentimental, baby-faced
creature with wings which so many pictures suggest. He is a
special messenger from God. *

### THE SEQUEL

And they delivered all these instructions briefly to Peter
and his companions. Afterwards Jesus himself sent out
by them from east to west the sacred and imperishable
message of eternal salvation.

When he had risen from the dead early on Sunday 9
morning he appeared first to Mary of Magdala, from
whom he had formerly cast out seven devils. She went 10
and carried the news to his mourning and sorrowful

11 followers, but when they were told that he was alive and
that she had seen him they did not believe it.

12    Later he appeared in a different guise to two of them as
13 they were walking, on their way into the country. These
also went and took the news to the others, but again no
one believed them.

14    Afterwards while the Eleven were at table he appeared
to them and reproached them for their incredulity and
dullness, because they had not believed those who had
15 seen him after he was raised from the dead. Then he said
to them: 'Go forth to every part of the world, and pro-
16 claim the Good News to the whole creation. Those who
believe it and receive baptism will find salvation; those
17 who do not believe will be condemned. Faith will bring
with it these miracles: believers will cast out devils in my
18 name and speak in strange tongues; if they handle snakes
or drink any deadly poison, they will come to no harm;
and the sick on whom they lay their hands will recover.'

19    So after talking with them the Lord Jesus was taken up
into heaven, and he took his seat at the right hand of God;
20 but they went out to make their proclamation everywhere,
and the Lord worked with them and confirmed their
words by the miracles that followed.

* But what happened next? In some manuscripts, the short
summary paragraph printed here immediately after verse 8*a*
is all that follows: in others, there are verses 9–20; others again
have both these endings. But it is widely agreed that neither
of them belongs to the original story, and that both represent
later attempts to fill a gap. Some hold that the Gospel was
originally meant to end at those words *for they were afraid*—a
highly dramatic climax, whose very abruptness and mysterious

refusal to say more stimulate the imagination: women, running, in abject terror! What had happened? But it is very doubtful whether the fear and terror would have suggested the believing awe which they would have to suggest if Mark had meant to end his Gospel on this note; and it is far more likely that the abruptness is merely due to the end of the book having been somehow torn or damaged, and that it did originally continue in some such way as Matthew does, with accounts of Jesus showing himself alive to his friends, and finally appearing majestically in Galilee (see verse 7). That the women are described as saying nothing to anybody (verse 8) clearly does not mean that they did not tell their experience to their close friends. It probably means no more than that they were too terrified and in too much of a hurry to stop and speak to anybody they chanced to meet between the tomb and wherever they were staying.

The short ending—the single paragraph printed as verse 8 *b* —very tersely identifies the preaching of the Gospel by the Christian Church with the activity of the risen Jesus himself, so completely is he one with his Church. It is quite likely that *briefly* was originally the title of this paragraph (meaning 'here is a brief, summary account'), and has now got into the wrong position.

The longer ending, 9–20, has interesting features of its own, but is, in part, a summary of other accounts. For 9–11, see John 20: 1–2; for 12–13, Luke 24: 13–32; for 15, Matt. 28: 19; for 19, Acts 1: 9. Its own peculiar features link it more closely with the literature of the post-New Testament period than with the period of Mark's Gospel. ✻

✻   ✻   ✻   ✻   ✻   ✻   ✻   ✻   ✻   ✻   ✻   ✻   ✻

And now that you have finished Mark, do you agree that (p. 2 above) it is neither a collection of sayings nor a biography but an announcement of good news? And if so, can you define the good news? For instance, would it be good news without the death? Would it be good news without the part of the story that follows the death? Would it be good news if it were simply the story of a very good man who was martyred? Would it be good news if it were a story told merely by a historian, and not by someone who was also a member of the Christian Church, through which, as Christians believe, Jesus, the Son of God, still speaks and acts? Would it be good news if it were confined to something that happened in Palestine nearly two thousand years ago?

# INDEX

*Abba*, 117
Abiathar for Ahimelech, 27
abomination of desolation, 106
access to the presence of God, 128
Adam, 85
Ahimelech, *see* Abiathar
Alexander and Rufus, 126, 130
allegory (*see also* parable), 32 f., 36, 90, 93 f.
Alphaeus, 25
Amasa, 119
Andrew, 30
angels, 12, 131
anger of Jesus, 28, 73
anointed, *see* Messiah
Antiochus Epiphanes, 106
Antipas, 64
apocalyptic, 101 ff., 107, 109
little apocalypse, 101 ff.
Apocryphal Gospels, 4
apostles (*see also* Twelve), 30, 52
Aramaic, 45, 58, 117, 126
Augustus, 49
authority, 22, 73, 93

bandits, 119, 127
baptism, Christian, 83
of infants, 79
the Baptist's, 9 f.
Baptist, *see* John
Barabbas, 124 f., 127
bar Kokhba, 107
Beelzebub, 32
ben Koseba, *see* bar Kokhba
Bethany, 112
betrayal of Jesus, 113
Blasphemy, 123 f.
breaking of bread, 115

Caesarea Philippi, 64 f., 70, 83
Caligula, 106
calling by Jesus, 14 f.
Calvary *or* Golgotha, 126

carpenter, Jesus as, 47
Celsus, 15
children, 74 f., 79
chosen People, 107 f.
Christ, *see* Messiah
Christians, 75
Church, the, 68
claims of Jesus, 30
cleanness and uncleanness, 21, 55 f.
cleansing of the temple, 89 f., 93
Clement of Alexandria, 5
cloud as presence of God, 69
clouds, 107
conflict in the ministry, 53
*corban*, 55 f., 98 f.
covenant, new, 115
Creator, God as, 41
cross, crucifixion, 67, 125
cup, 83, 127
and bread, 115 f.
cures (*see also* miracles), 15 f., 17, 48, 62 f., 85
of blind, 62 f., 85
of deaf and dumb, 58 f.
of epilepsy, 72 f.
by exorcism, 17 f.
of haemorrhage, 44 f.
(raising) of Jairus' daughter, 45 f.
of leper, 21 f.
of paralysed man, 22
by spittle, 58, 63
curtain of the temple, 127 f.

David, 27, 33
son of, 85, 99
Dead Sea, 106
Scrolls, 8
death of Christ, the, 83, 84 f., 115, 127, 130
death, raising from, 45 f.
Decapolis *or* the Ten Towns, 43, 58
demons, demonic, evil spirits, 17 f., 32, 42, 48, 72, 106, 129